OCR HISTORY A

The First Crusade and the Crusader States 1073–1130

OCR and Heinemann are working together to provide better support for you

1002

www.heinemann.co.uk
✓ Free online support
✓ Useful weblinks
✓ 24 hour online ordering

0845 630 33 33

Part of Pearson

Heinemann is an imprint of Pearson Education Limited, a company incorporated in England and Wales, having its registered office at Edinburgh Gate, Harlow, Essex, CM20 2JE. Registered company number: 872828

www.heinemann.co.uk

Heinemann is a registered trademark of Pearson Education Limited

Text © Toby Purser

First published 2010

13 12 11 10 09

10 9 8 7 6 5 4 3 2 1

British Library Cataloguing in Publication Data

A catalogue record for this book is available from the British Library

ISBN 978-0435312695

Edited by Jane Anson
Designed by Pearson
Typeset by Saxon Graphics Ltd, Derby
Original Illustrations by Saxon Graphics Ltd, Derby
Cover design by Bigtop Design Ltd
Cover photo © Heritage Image Partnership/E&E Image Library
Printed in Spain by Graficas Estella

Acknowledgements
Photos and images
The author and publisher would like to thank the following individuals and organisations for permission to reproduce photographs:

Figures 1.1, 1.3, 1.4, 1.6, 3.2, 4.1, 4.2, 5.1, 6.1, 7.1, 8.1, 10.1, 10.2: Saxon Graphics Ltd; Figure 1.2: Alamy/The Print Collector; Figure 1.5: Getty/Lonely Planet Images; Figure 1.7: Alamy/Photos 12; Figure 2.1: Art Archive/Hagia Sophia, Istanbul/Alfredo Dagli Orti; Figure 2.2: Rex Features/Ettan Simanor/Robert Harding; Figure 2.3: Alamy/North Wind Pictures; Figure 3.1: Alamy/The London Art Archive; Figure 3.3: Getty Image Bank Images; Figure 4.3: Alamy/The London Art Archive; Figure 4.4: Alamy/Photos 12; Figure 6.2: Alamy/Imagebroker; Figure 6.3: Art Archive/Archives Nationales, Paris/Kharbine-Tapabor/Coll. Jean Vigne; Figure 7.2: Bibliothèque Nationale de France; Figure 7.3: Alamy/The Print Collector; Figure 8.2: Alamy/Mary Evans Picture Library; Figure 9.1: Bibliothèque Nationale de France; Figure 9.2: Alamy/Israel Images; Figure 10.3: Alamy/The London Art Archive; Figure 10.4: Alamy/Photos 12.

Written sources
The author and publishers wish to thank the following copyright holders for permission to reproduce the following extracts:

p.19, p.77 Source D, J. Phillips, *The Crusades 1095–1197*, Pearson Education; p.23 Source G, p.30 H.E. Mayer, *The Crusades*, OUP; p.41, Source B, T. Ashridge, *The First Crusade: a new history*, Simon and Schuster, UK; p.67 Source J, Jean Richard, *The Crusades c.1071–c.1291*, CUP.

Every effort has been made to contact copyright holders of material reproduced in this book. Any omissions will be rectified in subsequent printings if notice is given to the publishers.

Contents

Notes for teachers

This book, *The First Crusade and the Crusader States 1073–1130*, is designed to support OCR's History A specification. It is divided into two units: F962 Option A, Study Topic 1 and F964, Option A, Study Topic 1. The chapters are closely linked to the Key Issues in Units F962 and F964, and focus on two types of historical skill required: Period Studies (Unit F962, Chapters 1–10) and Enquiries (Unit F964, Chapters 1–6).

Period Studies

In the OCR examination, candidates are required to explain, analyse and assess and to consider the relationships between the key features, and there are opportunities to develop these skills throughout the book.

Students examine historical terms and concepts, learn to analyse a range of factors and judge their importance. Students should be developing skills to cross-reference, link, and compare the relative importance of factors for higher level answers. Most importantly, students need to think about making their own supported judgements about the relative importance of factors and the success and failure of each Crusade.

The activities will encourage a cumulative approach leading to summative questions such as 'bearing all this in mind, why did this happen?'

Enquiries

In the OCR examination, candidates are required to compare sources as evidence, and there are opportunities to practise this skill throughout the book.

Candidates also have to use a set of sources to evaluate an interpretation. In order to help develop the skills of interpreting sources, applying their own knowledge to assess the sources, and reaching a conclusion about the issue to which the sources relate, there are exercises which are stepped in difficulty. As a result, not all of the activities are in the format of the OCR papers, but they all aim to lead students towards the critical consideration of a set of four or five sources.

Help is given with identifying issues that candidates are likely to have to discuss. Though historians' views have been included, the AS paper is not focused on historiography or the different interpretations of historians, but on issues in which evidence may conflict.

Exam support

There is detailed exam preparation and support in the Exam Café on pages 130–149.

Exam Café focuses on the type of questions assessed in the exam in either Period Studies or Enquiries. It is divided into three areas:

- **Relax and prepare** is an area for sharing revision tips.
- **Refresh your memory** is an area for revising content.
- **Get the result** includes exam advice, plus sample questions and student answers with examiner comments and tips on how to achieve a higher level answer.

The First Crusade and the Crusader States 1073–1130 has been written specifically to provide teachers and students with a taught course that exactly reflects the key issues and skills in the specification topics. Each chapter begins with key questions on a key issue, which are then discussed in sequence, with supporting activities.

Additionally, each chapter includes a timeline that gives an overview of the chapter's chronology and a final review of what has been learnt, together with some review questions to help students' self-assessment of their knowledge.

Methods of assessment

The AS GCE is made up of two units. Candidates can do either Units F961 and F964 or F962 and F963. Centres choose one or two study topics from each unit. This book supports one unit in F962 and one unit in F964. They cannot be taken together.

The paper for F962 (and F961) is an essay question (Period Studies) paper. It will be assessed by two answers, each of which might be drawn from one or more than one key issue. Candidates can answer from a choice of three essay questions from one or two study topics. Each question is worth a maximum of 50 marks.

F963 (and F964) are document studies (Enquiries) papers. Four or five unseen sources are set for each exercise. The question paper contains a two-part document study question for each study topic. Candidates answer one question from the study topic they have studied. Question (a) is worth 30 marks and question (b) is worth 70 marks.

Each paper is 1.5 hours long and is 50% of the total AS GCE marks.

Notes for students

This book has been written to support you through the OCR A AS GCE History course. *The First Crusade and the Crusader States 1073–1130* will help you to understand the facts and concepts that underlie the topics you are studying. It can be used as a reference throughout your course.

You should refer back to this book during your revision. The Exam Café section at the end of the book will be helpful as you prepare for your exam.

The book makes use of the following features:

Key questions

Each chapter opens with some Key Questions. The content of the chapter will help you to find answers to these.

> **Key Questions:**
>
> In this chapter you will learn:
> - How important the Christian Church was in medieval Europe
> - How the Muslim world had expanded
> - What the Holy Roman and Byzantine Empires consisted of
> - How the papacy had developed in the eleventh century

Sources

We have included sources throughout the book to allow you to practise your historical skills. *Note*: the sources tend to be longer than they would be in the exam.

> **Source**
>
> (B) From Urban's speech at Clermont in 1095, reported by Baldric of Bourgueil (written 1108):
>
> *Christian blood, which has been redeemed by the blood of Christ, is spilled and Christian flesh, flesh of Christ's flesh, is delivered up to execrable abuses and appalling servitude…*

Activities

The activities have been designed to help you understand the specification content and develop your historical skills. Key activities are marked as either Period Studies or Enquiries and also in the top corner of each page with a P or an E.

> **ACTIVITY**
>
> Using the map on page 7 and your own knowledge, draw up a table of the Christian and the Muslim countries that had emerged by 1095.

Information

You should be thinking like an historian throughout your history course. These highlight content to provide extra detail to the main questions in the chapter.

> **Seljuk Turks**
>
> The Seljuks (or Seljuqs) had migrated from the eastern steppes of Turkestan in the tenth century. They had assimilated with Persian Islamic culture and religion under their first great leader, Seljuk. They were Sunni Muslims and extended their power right across the eastern Islamic world. Seljuk's grandson, Alp Arslan, defeated and captured the Byzantine Emperor Romanos IV. His son was Malik Shah, who consolidated his father's victories over the Byzantines in Anatolia.

Biographies

Biographies provide useful background information about key people who feature in the text.

> **BIOGRAPHY**
> **Muhammad the Prophet**
>
> A merchant from Mecca who by the time of his death in 632 had united the Arabian peninsula under the new Islamic religion. During the two centuries that followed, his successors, the **caliphs**, conquered Syria, Egypt, the Persian Empire (modern Iraq, Iran and

Case studies

Case studies are used to further illustrate the main questions. Most of the examples can be applied in some way to the topic you are studying for your AS exam.

Case study: the pilgrimage of Swegn Godwinsson (1051/2)

Swegn was the eldest son of Earl Godwin of Wessex, the most powerful man in England after the King, Edward the Confessor. Swegn had a notorious violent streak and after abducting a nun from Leominster and keeping her as a sex slave, he was banished from the royal court. After some years he returned, but very soon murdered his cousin Beorn. After this, the King declared him *nithing*, outcast and outlaw. Swegn clearly had a conscience, because he chose to go to Jerusalem on the pilgrimage to atone for his sins and died on the journey. He was not a pleasant character, but even he saw the pilgrimage as a path to redemption.

Definitions

Definitions of new words can be found in the margin next to where the word appears in the text to help put the word in context. All definitions can also be found in the Glossary (page 151).

rapine
Violent theft of another person's property.

Exam support

In our unique Exam Café on pages 130–149 you'll find ideas to help you prepare for your exams. You can **Relax** because there's handy revision advice

from fellow students, **Refresh your memory** with summaries and checklists of the key ideas you need to revise and **Get the result** through practising exam-style questions, accompanied by hints and tips on getting the very best grades.

Introduction

In November 1095, Pope Urban II preached a holy war against the unbelievers who had assaulted and destroyed the Christian churches in the east. He told those who joined the war that their reward would be everlasting life in heaven. The response to his appeal was extraordinary: tens of thousands of people, armed and non-combatant, set off from France, Germany, Italy and northern Europe on the pilgrimage to Jerusalem. Their aim was to free the Christian churches in the Middle East from Muslim control. They travelled on foot or on horseback, and the journey took over three years. Most of the pilgrims died en route from disease and from savage fighting with enemies encountered along the way. Finally, in July 1099, the exhausted remnants of the Christian forces arrived at Jerusalem and, after a short siege, captured the city and slaughtered everyone inside its walls.

The First Crusade not only recaptured Jerusalem for the Christian Church, it also created a new kingdom centred around Jerusalem and extending over a hundred miles to the north. The kingdom was ruled by the king of Jerusalem and a network of princes and noblemen, following the system of the kingdoms of western Europe from which the crusaders had come. It was defended by the few committed professional troops who remained behind after capturing Jerusalem. They were supported by reinforcements from Europe, who garrisoned the newly built castles. In addition, the new Templar and Hospitaller military orders – fighting monks – defended the kingdom.

The unprecedented invasion of the Muslim world by pilgrims and warriors from Europe unleashed a Christian holy war onto the Middle East, and the military orders represented a permanent fighting force of holy warriors never seen before. However, the survival of the crusader kingdom was precarious, and shortage of men was a constant problem. A further threat was growing Muslim unification under the banner of Muslim holy war – the jihad. The jihad was not halted by the Second Crusade in 1148, and it eventually overwhelmed the crusader kingdom in 1187 when Jerusalem fell to the Muslim leader, Saladin, and his army.

The response of the West was to launch a Third Crusade, the greatest yet, led by the best military commanders of the day: Richard I of England and Emperor Frederick of Germany. The crusade had now become a matter not for pilgrims but for professional soldiers. Muslim unity, which had not existed in 1095, now demanded that the crusaders engage in total war against the combined military forces of Egypt, Syria and Turkey. The Third Crusade failed to recapture Jerusalem, but it did manage to regain coastal ports and leave a foothold in the region for future crusaders from Europe to exploit. The situation in 1193 was one of stalemate: the Muslims held Jerusalem, but the crusaders were to remain in the region for another century.

Timeline of the Crusades

1071	Seljuk Turks defeat the Byzantine army at the Battle of Manzikert.
March 1095	Envoys from the Byzantine Emperor Alexius Comnenus ask Pope Urban II for military aid.
27 November 1095	Pope Urban II launches the First Crusade at the Council of Clermont.
15 July 1099	Crusaders capture Jerusalem.
December 1144	Edessa falls to Zengi of Aleppo.
1 December 1145	Pope Eugenius III issues the *Quantum praedecessores* crusade appeal, launching the Second Crusade.
May–June 1147	Crusader armies from France, Flanders and Germany depart for the Second Crusade.
October 1147	German army defeated in Asia Minor.
June 1148	Council of Palmarea decides to attack Damascus; the siege fails, ending the Second Crusade.
4 July 1187	Battle of Hattin; Christian army wiped out by Saladin, King Guy captured.
October 1187	Fall of Jerusalem; Third Crusade launched by the pope.
7 September 1191	Battle of Arsuf; Richard I defeats Saladin.
October 1191	First march on Jerusalem turns back.
June 1192	Second march on Jerusalem fails.
5 August 1192	Battle of Jaffa; Richard I defeats Saladin.
September 1192	Truce arranged; Richard leaves in October, ending the Third Crusade.

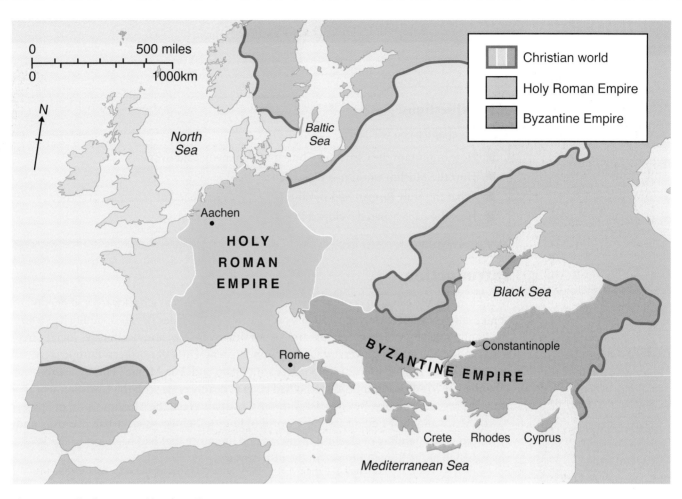

Figure 1.1   The Christian world in about AD 1050.

What were the boundaries of medieval Europe on the eve of the First Crusade?

> ## Key Questions:
>
> In this chapter you will learn:
>
> - How important the Christian Church was in medieval Europe
> - How the Muslim world had expanded
> - What the Holy Roman and Byzantine Empires consisted of
> - How the papacy had developed in the eleventh century

Introduction

Europe in the late eleventh century has traditionally been seen as a backward and deeply conservative peasant society, governed by established hierarchies (levels of authority) who frequently ruled by violence. Schools and universities were few, and healthcare, social care, roads and public buildings were practically non-existent. Parts of northern Europe were overpopulated. The Mediterranean borders with Spain and Asia Minor (Turkey) were inhabited by Muslim communities who had been at deadly odds with the Christian world since the seventh century. By contrast with the Christian West, the Muslim world of Spain, North Africa and the Middle East was a world of libraries, universities, urban planning and advanced understanding of classical medicine and literature that had been lost to the West since the fall of the Roman Empire in the fifth century.

The political kingdoms of England, France and the Germanic principalities owed spiritual allegiance to the head of the Catholic Church in Rome: the pope. Traditionally, the popes had been a highly influential but peaceful force in Europe. During the eleventh century, however, the papacy began to develop into a more politically active and aggressive power. The Greek Church was headed by the patriarch in Byzantium, also known as Constantinople (modern Istanbul). The Greek Church was also Christian, but followed a different set of beliefs from those of the Catholic Church. When the threats from Muslim incursions into Turkey became serious, the Byzantine emperor approached Pope Urban II in Rome in 1095 to seek help in combating the Muslims, and so it was the papacy in Rome that was ready to take the lead in Europe.

Boundaries of the mind: mortality and mentalities

Average life expectancy in Europe in the late eleventh century was around 30 years, the infant mortality rate was 50 per cent and chances of surviving childhood were poor. Diet was basic, malnutrition was common, and starvation was all too frequent in times of bad harvests. From age thirteen until they reached menopause in their late thirties, girls and women could expect repeated pregnancies, each one fraught with danger from blood loss, shock and infection. Boys and girls were likely to suffer deadly infection well into their teens, and the best most boys could expect was a working life of backbreaking toil on a minimal diet. The damp, cold climate of northern Europe did nothing to lessen the misery of sharing a small, dark house made of mud, wattle and thatch with the family's livestock and the extended family. The working day was determined by the hours of daylight and most of these were spent farming the land owned by the local lord.

KEY ISSUES

- Boundaries of the mind: mortality and mentalities
- Physical boundaries: Europe and the Mediterranean
- How had the papacy changed in the period 1073–95?

Viking

A general term applied to the pagan warriors who sailed from Norway, Sweden and Denmark to pillage, plunder and raid the wealthy and peaceful lands of France and England from the end of the eighth century to the early eleventh century. Some settled in northern France from 911, and their (Christian) descendants were the Normans who conquered England in 1066.

Contemporaries saw society as being organised into three levels, or 'orders': those who fought, those who prayed and those who worked, a system ordained by God and decided by one's birth. This structure of society, with the king at the top and the peasants at the bottom, was a simplification made by contemporaries. Medieval society actually consisted of a variety of farmers, smallholders in the countryside and merchants in the towns and cities. The many skilled workers, tradesmen and craftsmen, along with the growing class of literate officials and academics in the new schools and universities, meant that medieval society was far more complex.

Historians have traditionally called the social system the 'feudal system', from the Latin *feudum*, or 'fief', meaning a grant of land. It developed in response to the terror of the **Viking** raids into France and England during the period 790–1020. Kings could **enfeoff**, or grant warlords land in return for their military support against the invaders; local warlords in turn granted parts of this land to soldiers (**knights**) who were fed by the peasants who worked the land. A sophisticated code of honour and a network of allegiances grew out of this, with the knights passing the land to their heirs in a **hereditary** system. In theory, the peasants were protected by the knights, but in practice they endured warfare, rape and pillage. Many crusaders took their knights with them in 1095 and organised the kingdom of Jerusalem according to feudal loyalties.

Recently, historians have revised this view as a false construct created by contemporaries and repeated by historians. The feudal sources concerned with legal transactions over property – based upon the fiefs of land – do not necessarily give a rounded view of society as a whole. There was no real system, rather a multitude of customs and practices developed at different times and in different places.

Source A

A description of an oath of to the Count of Flanders, 1127.

First … the Count asked if he was willing to become completely his man, and the other replied, 'I am willing' and with clasped hands, surrounded by the hands of the Count, they were bound together by a kiss. Secondly, he who had done homage gave his fealty to the representative of the Count in these words, 'I promise on my faith that I will in future be faithful to Count William, and will observe my homage to him completely against all persons in good faith and without deceit.' Thirdly, he took his oath to this upon the relics of the saints.

From Galbert de Bruges, *Chronicle of the Death of Charles the Good.*

Source B

The German Emperor Henry IV confirmed a grant of the tolls to the monastery of St Simeon at Coblenz (1104). The right to collect tolls could be granted in the same way as the right to hold a fief.

Bakers of that place, whoever they be, or wherever they be, who sell bread there will give one loaf to the toll-gatherer every Sunday, or one obole every fourteen days.

Also, the tax of shoemakers coming from elsewhere will be given to them from Lady Day up to Martinmas. But for this they will give the toll-gatherer and eight monks a good banquet. But the toll-gatherer will give them six sets of wine, and a cheese which can be carried in one hand.

enfeoff

The act of granting land from the king or a nobleman to a knight was called enfeoffment. The land granted by this act was commonly known as a fief.

knights

The class of warriors who held land from the king and the Church.

hereditary

Titles and land were inherited in the Middle Ages. A man could acquire land by marriage, but it was rare to marry an heiress without being of the same social status and level of wealth. Intermarriage preserved the elite class of landowners and passed on land from father to son by inheritance. If a man died without sons, then his nephews, brothers or cousins inherited.

ACTIVITY
Period studies

Study Sources A and B.

1   Explain in your own words what is happening in Source A. Why does this fit the classic view of the feudal system?

2   Why does Source B present an alternative view of the simple feudal society of the three orders? What does it tell you about the economy?

1 What were the boundaries of medieval Europe on the eve of the First Crusade?

Figure 1.2   The three orders of medieval society: from left to right, the cleric, the knight and the peasant.

confess

Each week, or more often if possible, medieval people would attend confession: they went to see a priest and told him about their evil or ungodly deeds or thoughts. The priest would forgive people's sins on God's behalf, often setting them some sort of punishment or penance.

paganism

Before the existence of Christianity, people in Europe worshipped many gods – gods of the air, fire, water and earth. Only when Christianity became the official religion of the Roman Empire in the early fourth century did paganism begin to decline. After the Roman Empire collapsed, Europe reverted to paganism again, but Rome itself remained Christian and by AD 700 the Church had succeeded in converting the pagans across Europe.

For a person born into the peasantry, there was no way out. The harshness of the daily grind was punctuated by the Christian calendar of saints' days and feasts, which lightened the peasants' load somewhat. God and the Church were omnipresent (all-knowing and all-seeing) in the life of medieval people. People believed that their every action, word and thought would be judged. The great glimmer of hope was getting to heaven after death. This offered the promise of everlasting happiness and equality, and freedom from the miseries of the earthly life. There were several ways of achieving this promise, including regular attendance at church to worship and to **confess** one's sins to the priest. However, going on a pilgrimage was the best way to cleanse one's soul of sin and pave the way to enter heaven. It was this factor that gave Pope Urban's summons to arms in 1095 the greatest appeal.

What was the papacy?

After the collapse of the Roman Empire in the late fifth century, Rome became the centre of the Christian Church, with its own bishop, or pope (*papa* – 'father'). Roman Christianity established and promoted its brand across western Europe in the sixth and seventh centuries. It wiped out **paganism** and forced the Celtic Christians in Ireland, Wales and Scotland to obey the pope in Rome. The popes increasingly looked towards England and France for military support and in 800 it was the pope who crowned Charlemagne the first Emperor of the Romans, ruling the area that is modern France and western Germany (see page 10). The relationship between popes, kings and emperors was mutually beneficial: rulers were able to claim that their authority came from God and in return they gave the popes military protection from danger.

BIOGRAPHY
Muhammad the Prophet

A merchant from Mecca who by the time of his death in 632 had united the Arabian peninsula under the new Islamic religion. During the two centuries that followed, his successors, the **caliphs**, conquered Syria, Egypt, the Persian Empire (modern Iraq, Iran and Afghanistan), northern Africa and most of Spain.

Physical boundaries: Europe and the Mediterranean

What was the Muslim world?

In the last quarter of the eleventh century, Christian Europe was bordered by Muslim states from southern Spain in the west, across the whole of North Africa, through Palestine to Asia Minor (modern Turkey) in the east. The main powers in Europe were France, the Holy Roman Empire and the Christian Byzantine Empire (see below), which consisted of modern Greece and the Balkans with its capital at Constantinople. The Mediterranean Sea was the barrier between the two world religions, Christianity and Islam. Founded by the prophet **Muhammad**, the Islamic religion had exploded onto the world in the late seventh century, advancing across the Christian principalities of North Africa, through Spain and into southern France, where it had been halted in the eighth century and pushed back into Spain.

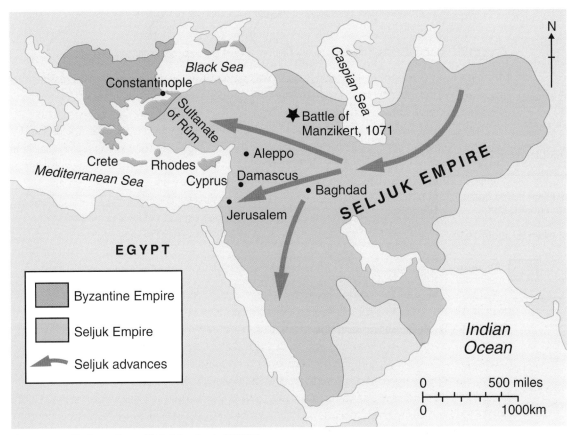

Figure 1.3   The Byzantine and Seljuk Empires in AD 1095.

It was in the east, however, where the Christian and Muslim worlds remained at flashpoint. In 1071 the Byzantine Empire suffered a major defeat at the hands of the **Seljuk Turks** at the **Battle of Manzikert** in Asia Minor. It was the increasing advances of the Seljuk Turks which prompted the Byzantine emperor to seek help from western Europe, appealing specifically to the Christian leader, the pope, who called for a holy war, or crusade, in 1095. It was this appeal that was to light a fire that raged between the Christian and Muslim worlds for the following five hundred years and that later became known as the crusades.

Seljuk Turks

The Seljuks (or Seljuqs) had migrated from the eastern steppes of Turkestan in the tenth century. They had assimilated with Persian Islamic culture and religion under their first great leader, Seljuk. They were Sunni Muslims and extended their power right across the eastern Islamic world. Seljuk's grandson, Alp Arslan, defeated and captured the Byzantine Emperor Romanos IV. His son was Malik Shah, who consolidated his father's victories over the Byzantines in Anatolia.

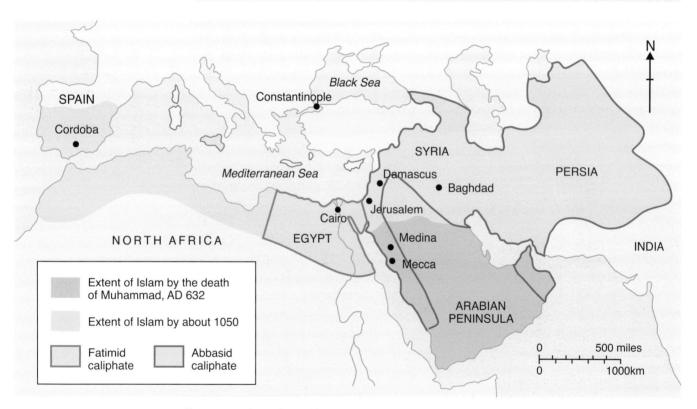

Figure 1.4   The Muslim world in about 1050.

Battle of Manzikert

The Battle of Manzikert was fought between the Byzantine forces and the Muslims, led by Alp Arslan, in August 1071 near Manzikert (modern Malazgirt in eastern Turkey). It resulted in one of the most decisive defeats of the Byzantine Empire and the capture of the Byzantine Emperor Romanos IV. The battle broke Byzantine resistance and prepared the way for the expansion of Turkish settlement in Anatolia.

What was the Byzantine Empire?

The Byzantine Empire grew out of the old eastern Roman Empire from the fifth century AD, gradually becoming Greek in culture. The Empire was the principal barrier to the Islamic armies that were advancing from the east, but by the later eleventh century it was dangerously weakened. The religion was Orthodox Christianity and was headed by the patriarch in Constantinople. The eastern church grew apart from the Roman western church and in 1054 the two split completely in the Great Schism. Attempts were made to heal the divide, and Urban's crusade of 1095 may have been a part of that effort, but the two Christian churches have remained separate.

The capital of the Byzantine Empire was Constantinople, named after the Roman Emperor Constantine who built it in the early fourth century. It rivalled Rome, becoming a city of fabulous palaces and streets, and controlling the trade routes between Asia and Europe and the Black Sea and the Mediterranean. By 1095 Constantinople was the frontier between the Islamic and Christian worlds, but it was not until 1453 that it was captured and established as the Ottoman Turks' capital, renamed Istanbul. Its city walls, dating from the time of Constantine, survive today.

caliph

A Muslim religious and political leader. The caliphs were Muhammad's successors.

ACTIVITY

Using the map on page 7 and your own knowledge, draw up a table of the Christian and the Muslim countries that had emerged by 1095.

Figure 1.5 The walls of the ancient Byzantine capital of Constantinople, now Istanbul.

P

1 What were the boundaries of medieval Europe on the eve of the First Crusade?

clerical marriage

Priests in the Catholic Church were forbidden to marry; their vows demanded that they remain celibate for life. However, many priests and bishops ignored this and had mistresses and children.

Church abuses

Many priests and bishops were also guilty of nepotism, that is, they were securing jobs in the Church for their family members, often their children. Other forms of corruption included selling church positions for money (simony); taking two or more church jobs at once (pluralism) and frequently not actually doing their job because they were elsewhere (absenteeism). A famous pluralist was Archbishop Stigand of Canterbury, who was also Bishop of Winchester; he was deposed in 1070.

What was the Holy Roman Empire?

After the collapse of the Roman Empire in the fifth century, Europe splintered into dozens of small states. However, by the late eighth century the kingdom of the Franks emerged as the most powerful, and in 800 their king, Charlemagne (Charles the Great) was crowned Emperor of the Romans by Pope Leo III. Charlemagne's empire covered the area that is modern France, Germany, Hungary and northern Italy. In 840 this empire was divided up and in 961 the German King Otto I was crowned emperor by the pope. German kings held the title 'Emperor of the Romans', which later became 'Holy Roman Emperor', for the next ten centuries. The Emperor of the Romans remained the premier royal leader of Europe, although the popes often had stronger links with the kings of France.

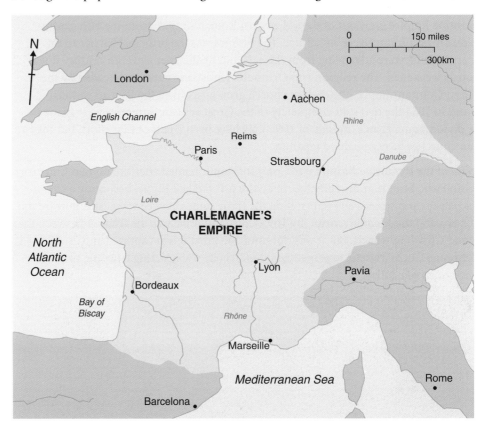

Figure 1.6   The empire of Charlemagne, the first Holy Roman Emperor, in AD 800.

How had the papacy changed in the period 1073–95?

The appeal from the Byzantine Emperor Alexius Comnenus to Pope Urban II in 1095 had a massive impact. This was partly because for several decades the papacy had been undergoing reform that amounted to an intellectual and political revolution in the Christian leadership of Europe. The reforming ideas began in the monasteries, particularly at **Cluny** in France. The reformers aimed to impose a more consistent interpretation of **St Benedict's Rule** and a more uniform commitment to discipline, prayer and study. Cluny had a huge influence on church thinking. Popes now wanted to see a clearer division between the sacred and the worldly in matters such as **clerical marriage**, and **church abuses** needed to be reformed. But more than this, popes such as Leo IX (1049–54) and Gregory VII (1075–85) wanted to impose their authority on kings and emperors in matters such as the **appointment of bishops**, and to assert the Church's role as a world political power. It was **Pope Urban II** (1088–99) however, who saw the appeal from Byzantium as an opportunity not only to assert papal authority over western Europe, but also to extend the power and influence of the Roman Church into the east.

appointment of bishops

A major source of discord between the Church and monarchs was the appointment of bishops, because bishops were so wealthy and powerful. Kings always wanted to appoint their own bishops, choosing men who would agree with royal policy. However, the pope in Rome saw it as his choice and could therefore appoint bishops who were loyal to Rome.

Figure 1.7   Pope Urban II consecrating the abbey church at Cluny, from a twelfth-century manuscript. The largest church in Europe throughout the Middle Ages, Cluny was almost totally destroyed in 1793, during the French Revolution.

Cluny

In 910 Count William I of Aquitaine founded the Abbey of Cluny in Burgundy, France. Within a hundred years the abbey was at the centre of a vast network of monasteries across Europe with close connections to the papacy. The monastic network was hugely influential both in the church and in politics, and produced many bishops, abbots and some popes, including Urban II. The Cluniac establishment was at the centre of the papal reforms during the later eleventh century.

St Benedict's Rule

St Benedict, founder of the monastery of Monte Cassino in Italy, wrote a rule in the sixth century (530–60) setting out the tenets of humility, silence and obedience for the monastic life. By the ninth century the Rule of St Benedict had become the standard rule by which monasteries were run, and the Benedictine order was the most influential at the time of the First Crusade.

ACTIVITY

Answer the following questions in a short paragraph, listing at least five points.

1 Why was the monastery of Cluny so important in the reforms of the eleventh century?

2 What were the church abuses that needed reforming?

3 Why was the appointment of bishops such an issue?

ACTIVITY

In groups, discuss the following question.

Does Henry IV's surrender at Canossa demonstrate more Henry's weaknesses as emperor or Gregory's strengths as pope?

Why was the Investiture Contest so significant?

In 1075, soon after he was elected pope, Pope Gregory VII declared that his authority was superior to that of all earthly rulers. This was a departure from the usual papal stance of purely spiritual superiority, when popes did not interfere with politics or military matters. Not surprisingly, this did not go down at all well with the political rulers of the day. Gregory clashed with the German Emperor Henry IV, causing civil war in Germany and exile for Gregory, in what was known as the Investiture Contest. The initial spark of this discord was the appointment of the Archbishop of Milan. Henry IV persuaded the German bishops to declare Pope Gregory deposed, and had an alternative pope installed. However, the German princes rebelled against Henry and in a dramatic scene, the Emperor had to travel through the Alps of northern Italy to the fortress town of Canossa, where he begged forgiveness from Gregory, standing for four days in public humility in the winter weather. Gregory granted Henry forgiveness and the event was greatly symbolic, since it at last placed the papacy at the heart of politics and put the developing ambitions of the reforming popes to the forefront.

Conclusion

The pre-conditions that prepared the ground for the First Crusade were established in the following ways:

- The Islamic world was fragmented into a number of small factions that were often at war with one another.

- From the fifth to the eleventh centuries, the Roman Empire was broken down into the feudal kingdoms of western Europe, based on a warrior society.
- The papacy, for so many centuries politically and militarily weak, now found a new voice in reforms that demanded actual, as well as spiritual, power.
- The struggling Byzantine Empire now needed to turn to the West for help against its Muslim neighbours.
- The power of the Cluniac monastic network and Pope Gregory VII's triumph over Emperor Henry IV at Canossa created a situation where the papacy was able to take the lead, which it did in 1095.
- Living conditions in medieval Europe were so miserable, and the teachings of the Catholic Church were so dominant in the minds of medieval people, that the call to the crusade in 1095 would appeal to many thousands of people.

Review questions

Answer the following questions in two to three paragraphs, or in the form of a list.

1 How did the papal reforms make an impact on the political leaders of Europe?

2 Was medieval society prepared for a holy war?

Why was the First Crusade launched?

Key Questions:

In this chapter you will learn:

- Why Pope Urban II turned Emperor Alexius' appeal for help into a papal crusade
- How the pilgrimage became an armed pilgrimage with spiritual rewards
- Why the concept of holy war was important

You will also develop the following skills:

- Assessing the language and tone of documents with reference to religious hatred and incitement to violence as a form of propaganda
- Understanding the nature of 'holy' and 'just' war
- Comparing sources and their limitations
- Understanding causation, a major historical concept
- Making a judgement on the papal motives for calling the crusade in 1095

Holy Land

The region that included Jerusalem – the Holy City where Jesus was crucified – and the towns of Bethlehem and Nazareth, plus the areas of Jordan and Galilee. All were held in high esteem by the Christian West.

Introduction

At Clermont in France on 27 November 1095, Pope Urban II preached a holy war against the 'heathens' and 'unbelievers' in the Middle East who were apparently responsible for the destruction of the Christian churches, especially the Church of the Holy Sepulchre in Jerusalem, site of the crucifixion. The response across western Europe was unprecedented; tens of thousands of people from all classes set out to liberate the **Holy Land** in a movement that was to become known as the crusades.

Chapter timeline

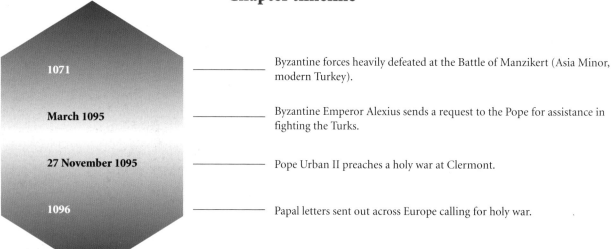

1071	Byzantine forces heavily defeated at the Battle of Manzikert (Asia Minor, modern Turkey).
March 1095	Byzantine Emperor Alexius sends a request to the Pope for assistance in fighting the Turks.
27 November 1095	Pope Urban II preaches a holy war at Clermont.
1096	Papal letters sent out across Europe calling for holy war.

The motives of the Pope were complex. He had received a request from the Byzantine Emperor Alexius I in Constantinople for help in fighting the Turks, but Urban had little intention of sending an army to help the Emperor. Urban's reasons for launching the crusade included the following, which were designed to increase the power of the papacy:

- The Investiture Contest (see page 12) had damaged the reputation of the papacy. Rome had been sacked by Norman troops in 1085 and Holy Roman Emperor Henry IV had installed an alternative pope, Clement III, to do his bidding.

- Rather than helping the Byzantine Empire, Urban wanted a Christian army to reconquer the Holy Land for Rome, and to extend Roman influence into the eastern Mediterranean.

- By launching a general invasion of the East, he would be seen to be the greatest leader in Europe, above princes and emperors.

- The papacy would now increase its political status in Europe, building on the reforms of previous popes and exploiting Pope Gregory's victory over Emperor Henry IV at Canossa in 1076.

- Urban's appeal for a crusade specifically targeted the nobility of France and northern Europe. This would divert the violence of the warring European kingdoms and principalities and create peace within Europe.

  - The nobles themselves had a variety of motives. These were chiefly spiritual, but desire for material gain and the acquisition of land were also important. Urban carefully orchestrated a propaganda campaign to whip up war-fever and appeal to the spiritual desire and fighting spirit of the nobles.

Urban deliberately drew on the established Christian tradition of the pilgrimage, but he also added the philosophy of the 'holy war', which justified the killing of other human beings. This thinking in western Christian theology was not new, but when it was combined with the political reforms of the papacy in the decades before the Council of Clermont, and Pope Gregory's victory over Emperor Henry IV at Canossa, and now the pilgrimage, it became explosive material indeed.

KEY ISSUES

- What help did Emperor Alexius request in 1095?

- What did Pope Urban II preach at Clermont in 1095?

- What were Urban II's aims in launching the First Crusade?

- How significant was the pilgrimage to Jerusalem?

- What was the 'holy war'?

Figure 2.1 The Byzantine Emperor Alexius Comnenus, whose appeal to Pope triggered the First Crusade.

What help did Emperor Alexius request in 1095?

In March 1095 Pope Urban held a council at Piacenza, Italy, to deal with matters of Church reforms. At the council, envoys sent from the Byzantine Emperor Alexius requested aid to help him fight off the Seljuk Turks who were ravaging Asia Minor, the borders of the Byzantine Empire. Alexius' request deliberately exaggerated the threat from the Muslims. It also mentioned Jerusalem, since he knew that any mention of the Holy City would be sure to attract the attention of the Christian West.

How threatened was the Byzantine Empire in 1095?

The Byzantines had been defeated in 1071 by Sultan Alp Arslan at the Battle of Manzikert in eastern Anatolia (modern Turkey). Under Sultan Malik Shah (1077–92) the Byzantines had been driven out of the eastern regions of Anatolia, and the Turks were now encroaching further west, towards the Byzantine capital of Constantinople itself. The death of Malik Shah and Emperor Alexius' treaty with Kilij Arslan in 1092 gave the Byzantine Empire much-needed breathing space. Alexius was hiring more and more soldiers from western and northern Europe. Norman warriors, the descendants of those Vikings who had settled in northern France, were the favoured mercenaries of the eleventh century. By 1095 therefore, the threat to the Byzantine Empire, although serious, was not necessarily as catastrophic as Alexius depicted it at the Council at Piacenza.

Were relations between Rome and Byzantium improving?

Alexius' request for help in 1095 also came in the context of improving relations with the papacy in the West. Urban II made efforts to communicate more effectively with Alexius, releasing him in 1089 from the excommunication under which Pope Gregory had placed him. Alexius responded positively and friendly relations were established.

rapine

Violent theft of another person's property.

razed

When something, usually a building, is completely demolished.

What did Pope Urban II preach at Clermont in 1095?

In November 1095, Pope Urban II held a council at Clermont, France. The topics discussed consisted mainly of church matters such as corruption, appointments, and the adultery of the King of France. However, on the last day of the Council of Clermont, 27 November, Urban made an extraordinary speech. In the fields outside the town, he addressed thousands of people, telling them of the slaughter and oppression of Christians in the East by the Muslims. He told them how churches had been attacked and damaged and how the rich and

Source

(A) There are four accounts of Urban's speech at Clermont. None of them is unquestionably reliable, as they were all written several years after the event and they differ from one another. However, they do agree on the supposed atrocities committed by the Muslims and on the urgent need for assistance from the West. This extract is taken from Robert of Rheims' account of Urban's speech (written before 1108):

… a foreign race, a race absolutely alien to God … has invaded the land of the Christians, has reduced the people with sword, **rapine** *and flame and has carried off some as captives to its own land, has cut down others by pitiable murder and has … completely* **razed** *the churches of God to the ground…*

the poor in the West could now help their brothers and end civil war in their own countries by going to the Holy Land. The response was massive; his speech was interrupted by shouts of 'God wills it!' and hundreds pushed forward to take the cross, cutting up garments in the shape of crosses and attaching them to their shoulders in imitation of Christ.

ACTIVITY

Enquiries

1   What does Source A mean by 'a race absolutely alien to God'?

2   According to Source A, what language does Urban use to stir people's emotions into fighting for the Holy Land?

What were Urban II's aims in launching the First Crusade?

Planning and papal propaganda

Although the popular response to Urban's speech was undoubtedly spontaneous, its preaching had been extremely well planned. The request from Alexius in March served as a useful tool and Urban exaggerated the horrors in the East just as Alexius had done in order to get the response he wanted. The speech at Clermont was a calculated attempt by Urban, a Cluniac reformer, to assert papal power and authority not only over western European leaders and people, but to assert the influence of Rome onto the Byzantine and Muslim East. At Clermont, **Bishop Adhemar of Le Puy**, who was to become the leader of the crusade, stepped forward to take the cross first; he knew exactly what Urban was going to say. The powerful Count of Toulouse, Raymond of St Gilles, sent messengers declaring his willingness to join the crusade on 1 December; again, he knew what Urban was planning before the speech. In the new year of 1096, Urban toured northern France to seek recruits, writing letters requesting support. His preaching coincided with saints' days and important festivals to guarantee a high turn-out.

BIOGRAPHY

Bishop Adhemar of Le Puy

The spiritual leader of the First Crusade, Adhemar was papal legate, which meant that he had full powers of the pope in the pope's absence. He died from disease after the capture of Antioch in 1098. After this, the leadership of the crusade passed into secular hands. Successive popes attempted to regain control of the crusading movement after this, but without success.

Source

B   **From Urban's speech at Clermont in 1095, reported by Baldric of Bourgueil (written 1108):**

Christian blood, which has been redeemed by the blood of Christ, is spilled and Christian flesh, flesh of Christ's flesh, is delivered up to execrable abuses and appalling servitude…

How significant was the pilgrimage to Jerusalem?

To medieval Christians, Jerusalem was the centre of the world: it was a site sanctified by the crucifixion, the main focus of the Christian religion. It was familiar to people through psalms, songs and **relics**, and they were taught that it would be the place of the Last Judgement for all Christians.

As well as exaggerating the horrors in the East, Urban carefully manipulated his appeal towards the recapture of Jerusalem. This turned out to be the greatest way of getting recruits. When Emperor Alexius mentioned the Holy City in his request for help, he had been fully aware that this would increase its appeal in the West, though his plan was simply to regain Byzantine territory in Asia Minor. Urban probably made no mention of Jerusalem in his speech at Clermont – the original speech talked of the restoration of the 'eastern churches' – but so great was the popular pressure that by 1096 Jerusalem had become the main goal. Very quickly then, either at or soon after Urban's speech, the aim of the crusade was Jerusalem, not, as Emperor Alexius had thought, to send a few thousand soldiers to Constantinople to help him regain land in Asia Minor.

By turning the objective towards Jerusalem, Urban was drawing upon a deep well of Christian belief: the pilgrimage. Completing a pilgrimage, to Rome, Santiago de Compostela (Spain) or Jerusalem, would grant the pilgrim remission of **penance**.

relic

A religious object such as the bones or clothes of a saint, or even part of the cross on which Jesus was crucified (the 'True Cross'). Touching or kissing a relic was believed to cure illness and cleanse sins. Holy relics were stored in ornate boxes known as reliquaries. If an oath was sworn over one of these it made the oath even more binding.

Figure 2.2   Jerusalem, the Holy City, is important to Christians, Jews and Muslims.

penance
It was believed that after death, entry to heaven was only granted to those whose souls were the purest. Purity was gained through acts of penance such as prayer, devotion to good works, and pilgrimages. All these increased a person's chances of getting to heaven.

Jerusalem was a magical place in the medieval Christian mind, the very pinnacle of Christian devotion. It was the place of the crucifixion of Christ. No other relics or holy sites – even Rome – could compete. The heavenly city had gates of sapphire, walls bright with precious stones – or so the Bible said. For most people, there was little distinction between the real city and the city of eternal bliss. It was for many heaven on earth – literally.

Sources

C   **From Pope Urban's speech at Clermont in 1095, reported by Baldric of Bourgueil (written in 1108):**

It ought to be a beautiful ideal for you to die for Christ in that city where Christ died for you [Jerusalem], but if it should happen that you should die here, you may be sure that it will be as if you had died on the way, provided, that is, Christ finds you in his company of knights...

D   **From Jonathan Phillips, *The Crusades, 1095–1197*:**

The holy city was such a potent image that the pope could not have used it as a decoy solely to help the Greeks and to facilitate a union with the Orthodox Church. It was the ideas of liberating the Christians of the Levant [the Middle East] and the city of Jerusalem that stirred the hearts and minds of those who planned the expedition and those who took the cross. Furthermore, by intending to recapture Christ's patrimony the crusade had a just cause, which ... was a prerequisite for the justification of Christian violence.

Phillips, J. (2002). *The Crusades, 1095–1197*. Harlow: Longman

ACTIVITY

Enquiries

1   Why does Source C say that if , when you die, 'Christ finds you in his company of knights' it will be the same as if you died on the way to Jerusalem? How would this encourage people to join the crusade?

2   Compare Sources C and D as evidence for the significance of Jerusalem as the crusade's destination.

Who went on the pilgrimage?

People had been going on pilgrimages to Jerusalem for centuries before Urban's speech at Clermont, ever since the year 333, when a pilgrim from Bordeaux reached Palestine. Christian pilgrimages to Jerusalem reached a peak in 1033, the millennium of Jesus' crucifixion. Jerusalem had become part of the Islamic world in the seventh century; it was a holy city to Islam because it was the site of Muhammad's ascension to heaven, but Christian pilgrims were allowed entry. Monasteries and hospices were built throughout Europe along the pilgrims' route. Pilgrimage was a way of doing penance for sins; it was dangerous and difficult, but the stream of pilgrims was continuous. Men of violence such as Fulk Nerra ('the Black'), Count of Anjou and Robert 'the Devil', Duke of Normandy, suddenly found themselves filled with remorse and guilt at the horrors of their violent lives, and set off to travel thousands of miles to Jerusalem. Fulk returned home to France, where he founded an abbey, but Robert died on the way back, leaving a seven-year-old son, who later became known as William the Conqueror, to become duke of Normandy.

Case study: the pilgrimage of Swegn Godwinsson (1051/2)

Swegn was the eldest son of Earl Godwin of Wessex, the most powerful man in England after the King, Edward the Confessor. Swegn had a notorious violent streak and after abducting a nun from Leominster and keeping her as a sex slave, he was banished from the royal court. After some years he returned, but very soon murdered his cousin Beorn. After this, the King declared him *nithing*, outcast and outlaw. Swegn clearly had a conscience, because he chose to go to Jerusalem on the pilgrimage to atone for his sins and died on the journey. He was not a pleasant character, but even he saw the pilgrimage as a path to redemption.

Why was the pilgrimage becoming more difficult?

The pilgrimage was seen as the climax to the Christian life on earth. However, by the middle of the eleventh century the journey to Jerusalem was becoming increasingly difficult now that much of Asia Minor and all of Palestine were part of the Muslim world. In 1009 the church of the Holy Sepulchre had been destroyed, and when Bishop Gunther of Bamberg led a party of 7000 pilgrims to Jerusalem in 1064 they were attacked by Muslims and had to defend themselves for several days. It was felt in the West that the time had come for new measures to protect and defend Christian pilgrims and the holy churches.

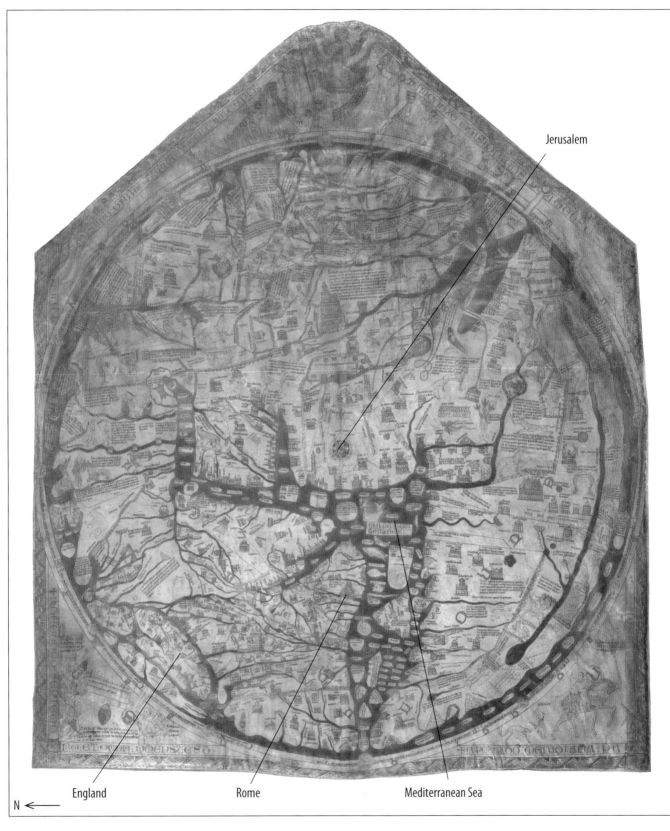

Jerusalem

England

N ←

Rome

Mediterranean Sea

Figure 2.3   The Mappa Mundi ('map of the world') dating from the later thirteenth century, shows Jerusalem at the centre of the world, reflecting the medieval world view.

Sources

(E) **Guibert of Nogent, writing before 1108, gives an account of Urban's speech at Clermont:**

If you consider that you ought to take great pains to make a pilgrimage to the graves of the apostles or to the shrines of any other saints, what expense of spirit can you refuse in order to rescue, and make a pilgrimage to, the cross, the blood, the Sepulchre? Now we are proposing that you should fight wars which contain the glorious reward of martyrdom, in which you can gain the title of present and eternal glory.

(F) **A letter from Pope Urban II to French counts and their knights (1096–99):**

No one must doubt that if he dies on this expedition for the love of God and his brothers his sins will surely be forgiven and he will gain a share of eternal life through the most compassionate mercy of our God.

ACTIVITY

Enquiries

1   What does Source E mean by 'the graves of the apostles'?

2   According to Source E, what was Urban offering to the pilgrims if they went to Jerusalem?

3   Compare Sources E and F as evidence for the rewards granted on the pilgrimage to Jerusalem. (See page 66 for guidance on comparing sources.)

What was the 'holy war'?

At Clermont, Pope Urban preached a holy war against the infidel (unbeliever). The idea of the holy war was not new. It had its roots in the 'just war' theory based on the defence or right to recover a rightful possession, a doctrine proposed by **St Augustine** 700 years earlier.

BIOGRAPHY

St Augustine of Hippo (354–430)

Born in North Africa, Augustine was a philosopher and theologian of profound importance in the history of western Christianity. He developed the view that the Church was a City of God, distinct from the City of Man. This view shaped medieval thinking for a thousand years.

Augustine's writings included works on original sin and just war. Just war, he proposed, required the authority of the state, it must occur for good and just purposes rather than self-gain, and love must remain a central theme even in the midst of violence. The Augustinian order of monks named themselves after Augustine, using a Rule based on his writings.

More recently than St Augustine, popes had begun to use the idea of holy war on several occasions:

- In the ninth century, Popes Leo IV and John VIII promised eternal life to Christians who fell in battle against the Arabs or the Vikings. This was a war against the heathen, an imperial duty to recover land and property that were rightfully theirs.

- In 1053, Pope Leo IX gathered an army to fight the Normans of Sicily who were attacking papal lands. Leo offered his German troops exemption from punishment for their crimes and remission of penance (it didn't help much – he was defeated and captured).

- In 1075, Pope Gregory VII had gathered a group of knights known as the *milites sancti Petri* (the knights of St Peter), to enforce papal policy. He also encouraged the Christians in Spain in their fight against the Muslims (the **reconquista**). Gregory had also had plans to lead an expedition to the Holy Land in 1074.

- More controversially, in 1066 Pope Alexander II gave his blessing to the Norman Conquest of England by sending a papal banner to Duke William of Normandy prior to his invasion. William argued that the English King Harold was a perjurer and usurper and that the English Church needed reform; the papal support was a huge morale booster and encouraged many thousands to join William's invading army.

The 'reconquista' (reconquest)

After the Muslims had been forced back into central Spain from France in the early eighth century, Christians had fought to recover all of Spain and Portugal. In 1085 a major advance had been achieved with the capture of the Muslim-held city of Toledo by King Alfonso VI of Leon-Castile. Progress was slow. Lisbon was captured in 1147, but it was not until the 1490s that the reconquest of Spain and Portugal was completed.

How radical a concept was the 'armed pilgrimage'?

At the Council of Clermont in November 1095, Pope Urban combined the long-established tradition of the pilgrimage to Jerusalem with the appeal for military aid from Emperor Alexius. The result was an innovative and radical combination of the pilgrimage and the military campaign to defend the Holy Land, perhaps the natural conclusion of the Cluniac reforms. From this combination arose the idea of the warrior pilgrim. Before 1095, pilgrims had been peaceful travellers on a journey of penitential prayer and salvation, but the crusaders carried weapons. The crusade was to be an armed pilgrimage, an idea formed out of centuries of pilgrimage. Indeed, medieval people had no word for 'crusade'; they simply called it the *peregrination* – pilgrimage – or the *iter in terram sanctam* ('journey into the Holy Land').

This was a radical concept. Both holy war and pilgrimage were well established, but Urban combined the two for the first time with great effect.

Source

 From *The Crusades*, by H.E. Mayer:

The crusader carried weapons. A crusade was a pilgrimage but an armed pilgrimage which was granted special privileges by the Church and which was held to be specially meritorious. The crusade was the logical extension of the pilgrimage.

Mayer, H. E. (1988). *The Crusades*. New York: Oxford University Press.

ACTIVITY

Enquiries

What does Source G mean by saying that the crusade was the 'logical extension of the pilgrimage'?

What was the Peace of God movement?

At Clermont, Pope Urban had had another reason for creating a holy war and sending many thousands of knights to fight in the Holy Land. The Church was determined to reverse what it perceived as the breakdown of society in many parts of western Europe. The papacy had made repeated attempts to make peace. Several accounts of Urban's speech at Clermont mention in detail the violence committed by Christians against fellow Christians. It was felt that Christians should stop fighting one another and unite against the infidel. The papacy had attempted to end the violence before 1095 in what was called the Peace of God movement, which reflected the growing papal intervention in political life. The Peace of God movement began around 1000 and attempted to stop the violence in several ways:

- Local nobility started making agreements not to attack churches, unarmed persons and clergymen.
- By 1040, fighting was forbidden on certain days of the week.
- 'Assemblies of peace' met to swear oaths to keep the peace, and 'leagues of peace' composed of clergymen and noblemen enforced those promises.
- At the heart of this was the monastery of Cluny, which was drawing the Church ever closer to the secular world, directing and channelling the forces of violence.
- For Pope Urban, a Cluniac monk, it seemed logical to take this idea one step further and send the violence out of Europe and into the Muslim Middle East.

Sources

(H) **From Guibert of Nogent, describing Pope Urban's speech at Clermont in 1095 and how he criticised the civil wars between Christian warriors (written before 1108):**

Until now you have fought unjust wars; you have often savagely brandished your spears at each other in mutual carnage only out of greed and pride, for which you deserve eternal destruction and the certain ruin of damnation! Now we are proposing that you should fight wars which contain the glorious reward of martyrdom, in which you can gain the title of present and eternal glory.

(I) **Pope Urban's speech at Clermont in 1095, from an account by Baldric of Bourgeuil (1108):**

You have strapped on the belt of knighthood and strut around with pride in your eye. You butcher your brothers and create factions among yourselves. This, which scatters the sheepfold of the Redeemer, is not the knighthood of Christ ... if you want to take counsel for your souls you must either cast off as quickly as possible the belt of this sort of knighthood or go forward boldly as knights of Christ, hurrying swiftly to defend the Eastern Church.

ACTIVITY

Enquiries

1 What does Source H mean by 'unjust wars'?

2 How does Urban attempt to put an end to the violence between Christian knights, according to Source H?

3 Compare Sources H and I as evidence for Pope Urban's appeal to the knights to fight in a holy war.

ACTIVITY

Period Studies

In groups, discuss the following question.

Were Pope Urban's aims mainly political or religious? Consider the following:

- The background of the Cluniac reforms and the papal ambitions to lead Europe

- The importance of the pilgrimage and the theory of holy war

- The feudal warlords and violence within Europe at this time.

Conclusion

The First Crusade grew directly out of the papal reforms of the mid-eleventh century and acknowledged the deeply-rooted warrior cult in western Europe. The tradition of the pilgrimage was long-established and so was the concept of holy war. Pope Urban II launched the First Crusade for the following reasons:

- A Cluniac reformer himself, Pope Urban looked back to the reforming popes Leo IX and Gregory VII. He seized the moment to capitalise on the perceived weakness of the Byzantine Empire and turn its appeal for aid to Rome's advantage.

- He knew the power of the pilgrimage and the potency of Jerusalem in the minds of the people, but he carefully targeted his appeal at recruiting members of the European nobility to go on the mission to recapture the Holy Land for the Church of Rome.

- As a nobleman, he knew that the appeal would arouse the enthusiasm of the warrior knights of France and Germany.

- As a man of God, he saw this as an opportunity to heal the evils of civil war in Europe and deflect the violence onto the Muslims in the east.

Review questions

Period Studies

1 Discuss in groups the extent to which Emperor Alexius's appeal for help gave Pope Urban an excuse to launch his own particular crusade.

2. Draw up a list of reasons to explain why the city of Jerusalem was so significant to the crusaders.

3. Explain how the 'armed pilgrimage' differed from previous holy wars.

Enquiries

4. Use your own knowledge to assess how far Sources A–H support the interpretation that Urban targeted the knights of Europe when he launched the First Crusade.

3

Why did so many people join the First Crusade?

Key Questions:

In this chapter you will learn:

- Why thousands of peasants and soldiers joined the First Crusade
- How the People's Crusade abused the appeal and was destroyed
- Why relations between the West and Byzantium were poor

You will also develop the following skills:

- Assessing the language and tone of documents
- Comparing sources and their limitations
- Understanding how the call to holy war affected society
- Applying your knowledge of feudal society to the documents
- Making a judgement on the motives of the first crusaders

Introduction

Pope Urban's carefully orchestrated propaganda campaign launched at Clermont used highly emotive language and whipped up war-fever. This resulted in a massive wave of recruits for the new holy war, either as armed pilgrims – the new knights of Christ – or as ordinary pilgrims, unarmed and on foot, men and women of all ages. Across Europe, some 60,000 people answered the call to defend the churches in the East and restore the Holy Sepulchre to Christian hands. This was a unique mass movement of spiritual passion that was never repeated. This mass of peasants, women, old men and children as well as the knights was more than Urban wanted for his objective to create a new kingdom of Jerusalem – and it was certainly more than Emperor Alexius of Constantinople had envisaged when he sent his letter requesting military aid in Asia Minor.

The reasons for such a mass of people leaving their homes and families were varied:

- People of all classes were motivated by religious fervour and by penitence for past sins. They also hoped for spiritual reward – Urban had promised that all who participated in the crusade would be exempt from earthly penance.
- Political reasons were important to the leaders, as representatives of the pope in the Holy Land. The papacy was increasing its political power, and it was good to be seen as its ally.
- Territory was important to some of the knights and princes who had nothing in Europe; others were attracted by the prospect of booty and plunder.

Sources

A **From the *Deeds of the Franks* [French] (anonymous, 1100):**

And when this speech had already begun to be noised abroad, little by little, through all the regions and countries of Gaul [France], the Franks, upon hearing such reports, forthwith caused crosses to be sewed on their right shoulders, saying that they followed with one accord the footsteps of Christ, by which they had been redeemed from the hand of hell.

B **From Albert of Aachen, writing around 1120:**

Bishops, abbots, clerics and monks set out; next, most noble laymen, and princes of the different kingdoms; then, all the common people, the chaste as well as the sinful, adulterers, murderers, thieves, perjurers and robbers; indeed, every class of the Christian profession, nay, also women and those influenced by the spirit of penance – all joyfully entered upon this expedition ...

ACTIVITY

Enquiries

1   Why did people sew crosses on their right shoulders, according to Source A?

2   How does Albert of Aachen set out the social orders of medieval people in Source B? Where does he place women?

3   What do Sources A and B tell us about the response to Urban's call to arms?

4   Compare Sources A and B as evidence for the popular appeal of the crusade. Remember to look at the dates when they were written, and who wrote them. Compare the content to see where they agree and where they differ.

KEY ISSUES

■ Who joined the First Crusade?

■ Who were the leaders of the First Crusade?

■ Who went on the 'People's Crusade'?

■ What was the response of Emperor Alexius to the main crusade?

Who joined the First Crusade?

Pope Urban specifically targeted the knights of France for the armed pilgrimage. His vision was of soldiers of Christ, recruited and led by the Church for the holy war, extending the boundaries of Christendom. Urban was from the nobility and he understood the aristocratic world very well; his call would appeal to the codes of honour and loyalty amongst the knightly classes. He also knew that the crusade needed professional military men, and not unarmed pilgrims, to defeat the Muslims in battle.

The problem of inheritance

Urban promised that those who went on the crusade would keep possession of any lands they conquered. The traditional view is that this especially appealed to the younger sons of noble families, because of the system of **primogeniture**. Northern Europe was experiencing rising population and constant food shortages. Younger sons of the nobility were a problem to society: they possessed no estates that would occupy their time and produce an income, and as nobles, they did not expect to work for a living. Something had to be found for them to do, and the crusade of 1095 was a solution.

primogeniture

In northern France, only the eldest son inherited the family lands. Other sons got nothing. They could go into the Church, marry an heiress or join a nobleman's household as a soldier. In this way, the family estate remained intact, rather than being divided amongst many brothers. A woman could only inherit her father's property if there were no male heirs, including cousins, which was rare.

The Norman Conquest of England

The Norman Conquest of England in 1066 had demonstrated that a wholesale redistribution of land ownership from one class of people – the Anglo-Saxon 'thegns' (landowners) – to another – the Norman knights – could be achieved in twenty years. William the Conqueror had gained approval for his invasion of England from Pope Alexander, which gave the invasion a sense of holy war. Certainly, some of the leaders of the First Crusade personified this desire for land and plunder. Notable examples were Robert, Duke of Normandy (son of William the Conqueror) and the Normans from southern Italy, Bohemond of Taranto and his nephew Tancred, one of eleven brothers – a classic example of younger sons of the nobility striving for a living.

Figure 3.1 This scene from the Battle of Hastings (1066) in the Bayeux Tapestry (made around 1075) shows exactly how the knights of the First Crusade would have looked in battle. They wore helmets and mail coats (hauberks), and carried swords, lances and shields.

The Normans in Italy and Greece

At the same time they were conquering England, Norman warriors were also engaged in warfare on the fringes of the Byzantine Empire. In 1071 they captured Bari in southern Italy, the last Byzantine stronghold, under the leadership of Robert Guiscard, before going on to attack the Greek mainland itself. Alexius had to request help from the Venetians, which promoted long-lasting Venetian commercial interests in the eastern Mediterranean. Robert Guiscard's eldest son was Bohemond, the most feared Norman warrior. He was besieging Amalfi when he took the cross, clearly seeing the crusade as an opportunity to extend his territory. The Normans went on to carve out a kingdom in southern Italy and Sicily by 1100.

How far were land- and fortune-hunting a reality?

Urban's appeal to the nobles was made in the knowledge that when a feudal lord took the cross, his armed followers – who could amount to several hundred, depending on the status of the lord – had no choice but to go with him. The traditional historians' view was that land-hunger and plunder were what motivated men to go on the crusade, but the lord had to provide them all with arms and armour and supplies for the journey, which was a ruinously expensive business. The cost of chain mail, armour, horses and weapons amounted to several years' income for most knights. To ease the financial burden, the expense was usually shared by the family networks of fathers, sons, brothers, uncles and cousins. An example of an entire family unit taking the cross was the Montlhéry family, who included the father, son, brother-in-law, and five nephews, one of whom went on to become King Baldwin II of Jerusalem.

As well as the huge financial cost, there was the potential danger to a crusader's home, lands and family during the crusade. The Church promised to protect a crusader's property in his absence, but in fact lands were seized, and property and family attacked. Wives and daughters were especially vulnerable in a society where women were seen as possessions and marriage was a means of acquiring property. News of the death of a crusader left his widow unprotected, and abduction was not uncommon.

The pilgrimage to Jerusalem would be far more arduous and dangerous than people expected. However, the crusaders did not see themselves as settlers, and most intended to return home once their job was done. The promise of land was an incentive to some, but it was the spiritual reward (see page 19 for information about penance), the **remission of sins** and the prospect of going to heaven (outlined in Chapter 2) that would propel tens of thousands of people across Europe and into the East over the next three years.

> **remission of sins**
>
> In Christianity, a priest's formal pronouncement of forgiveness of the sins of a person who has expressed repentance. For the crusaders, the act of taking the cross and going on the crusade was an expression of repentance.

ACTIVITY

Enquiries

Use your own knowledge to assess how far the sources on page 30 support the interpretation that crusaders were motivated by a place in heaven.

ACTIVITY

Period Studies

How important a reason was material gain (land, plunder and wealth) to the crusaders?

Sources

C This charter (agreement) between brothers Odo and Bernard with the Abbey of Cluny illustrates the dangers of the crusade and also the threat to their property during their absence.

We, Bernard and Odo, brothers, for the remission of our sins, setting out with all the others on the journey to Jerusalem, have made over for 100 solidi [gold coins] to Artald, deacon of Lordon, a manor known as Busart ... We are making this arrangement on the condition that if, in the course of the pilgrimage that we are undertaking, because we are mortal and may be taken by death, the manor, in its entirety, may remain under the control of St Peter and the monastery of Cluny. ... If, however, another lays claim to this gift, not only is it protected from that which is sought, but may he suffer every curse and perpetual excommunication from God and the holy apostles for his sins ...

Charter from the Abbey of Cluny, 1096 (translated by J. Phillips)

D This charter shows not only Duke Odo's motivation for going on the crusade, but also his awareness of the possibility that he may not return and his preparations for death.

We wish it to be known to those present and to those of future generations that Duke Odo of Burgundy, fired by divine zeal and love of Christianity, wishes to go to Jerusalem with all the others of the Christians, but before setting out, it should be clearly known that if, at the end of his journey, his strength does not enable him to return with the multitude, then after his death, whenever it is known, he has granted to God and to St Mary the village of Marcenay, to be held in hereditary possession.

Charter from the Abbey of Molesme, c.1100 (translated by J. Phillips)

E Anna Comnena was the daughter of Emperor Alexius. She was deeply suspicious of the crusaders generally, convinced that their motives were greed and a desire to capture Constantinople.

Others of the Latins [crusaders], such as Bohemund and men of like mind, who had long cherished a desire for the Roman Empire [Byzantium], and wished to win it for themselves, found a pretext in Peter's preaching, as I have said, deceived the more single-minded, caused this great upheaval and were selling their own estates under the pretence that they were marching against the Turks to redeem the Holy Sepulchre.

Anna Comnena's *Alexiad* (Book 10), written around 1100

F From H.E. Mayer, *The Crusades*:

Naturally not all crusaders were moved by piety. In the Middle Ages too there were sceptics and the motives for going on crusade were many, various and tangled, often social and economic in character. But the offer of indulgence must have had an irresistible attraction for those who did not doubt the Church's teaching, who believed in the reality of the penalties due to sin ... such believers must have made a up a great part of those who went on the First Crusade.

Mayer, H.E. (1988). *The Crusades*. New York: Oxford University Press.

Who were the leaders of the First Crusade?

Urban addressed his appeal to the senior nobility of western Europe, specifically to those in France and Flanders. No king was asked to lead the crusade because this was a papal expedition. The political leaders in northern Europe were not united in the face of a common religious foe. The Holy Roman Emperor Henry IV, although he had submitted to Pope Gregory at Canossa in 1076, was still excommunicated and was not invited on the crusade. Urban did not invite King Philip I of France along to the party either, because

BIOGRAPHIES

Godfrey of Bouillon

Godfrey was a member of one of the most ancient and senior families of Europe, descended from Charlemagne. He was offered the throne of Jerusalem in 1099 but refused, becoming instead 'Advocate of the Holy Sepulchre'. He died in 1100, a year later.

Baldwin of Boulogne

A tall man and a great warrior, Baldwin was the brother of Godfrey of Bouillon. He founded the county of Edessa on the way to Jerusalem in 1098, and became king of Jerusalem on his brother's death in 1100. He extended the boundaries of the kingdom into the Transjordan and captured several cities on the coast.

Count Hugh of France

Brother of King Philip I of France, Hugh was shipwrecked on the way to Constantinople. He was rescued by the Byzantine imperial troops and kept under house-arrest until he agreed to swear the oath to the emperor. Hugh died at Tarsus in 1101 whilst campaigning against the Turks.

Duke Robert of Normandy

Eldest son of William the Conqueror, Robert inherited Normandy but his younger brother William became king of England. Robert was nicknamed 'curt-hose' (short-arse) and never lived up to his father's legendary status. He proved to be a successful crusader, but on his return to Normandy in 1100 he went to war against his brother Henry, who had seized the throne of England. Robert was captured by Henry in 1106 and imprisoned until his death in 1134.

Robert of Flanders

A leading nobleman who was with the crusade all the way to Jerusalem and returned with honour to Europe in 1100.

Stephen of Blois

Son-in-law of William the Conqueror by his marriage to William's daughter Adèle, Stephen proved to be weak. He deserted the crusade at Antioch but was sent back by his formidable wife, only to be killed in a battle in 1102. His son Stephen was king of England from 1135 to 1154.

Raymond of Toulouse (later known as Raymond of Tripoli)

Raymond was a senior leader of the military crusade and a close associate of Pope Urban. He intended never to return to France and established the county of Tripoli in the north of the kingdom after the capture of Jerusalem. He died in 1105.

Bohemond of Taranto

The most feared and famed warrior of the crusade. Bohemond was a Norman from southern Italy who had already been at war with the Byzantine Empire in the 1080s. Tall, with a broad chest and strong arms, he terrified Constantinople. In 1098 he set up the principality of Antioch, not bothering to complete the pilgrimage to Jerusalem. He was at war with the Greeks again in 1108 and died in southern Italy in 1111.

Philip had been excommunicated in 1094 for throwing his wife out of the family home. The king of England, William II, was busily consolidating his father's conquest and was very little inclined towards Church reforms (quite the opposite: he was homosexual, which was a grave sin in the eyes of the Church, and frequently left church appointments open so as to get extra income). Such division did not bode well for the Christian world as a whole. However, it actually suited Urban's purposes because it enabled him to set himself above the nobles of Europe without fear of a royal or imperial rival.

The men whom Urban invited to join the crusade included some of the greatest nobles of northern Europe, such as **Godfrey of Bouillon**, Duke of Lorraine; his brother Count **Baldwin of Boulogne**; **Count Hugh**, brother of the King of France; **Duke Robert of Normandy** (son of William the Conqueror); Count **Robert of Flanders**; Count **Stephen of Blois**; Count **Raymond of Toulouse** and the Norman-Sicilian **Bohemond of Taranto**.

Who went on the 'People's Crusade'?

Although Urban's appeal was specifically addressed to the nobility of Europe, the reality of the crusade was different. Of the 60,000 people who set out on the crusade in 1096, only 6000 (10 per cent) or so were knights. After Urban's speech at Clermont, preachers went out all across Europe and began to preach that those who took up the Cross would have all their sins remitted for eternity. This was rather more than Urban had actually offered, which was that earthly penance rather than total penance after death would be remitted. Urban tried to limit the appeal of the crusade to the south-west, central and northern areas of France, whilst persuading those in the south-east to remain behind to defend Christendom. (It would be unwise for all the leaders to depart, leaving no one to repel possible counter-attacks from the Muslim world.) The preachers spread the message far and wide, sometimes taking over the agenda entirely. The best-known of these was Peter the Hermit, a Frenchman who preached in northern France and into the German territories with great success.

> ### Source
>
> Guibert of Nogent, *History of Jerusalem*, 1108:
>
> *The common people became followers of a certain Peter the Hermit. Unless I am mistaken, he came from Amiens in France, and had led the life of a hermit. He travelled through cities and towns to preach, and was surrounded by such crowds of people, given such gifts, and so acclaimed for his holiness, that I remember no one ever having been held in such honour. Whatever he did or said was regarded as divine.*

anti-Semitic

Showing hostility or prejudice towards Jews (Semites). Attacks, or pogroms, fired hatred towards the Jews of central Europe which raged on and off for hundreds of years, reaching a dreadful climax in the Holocaust in the twentieth century.

These preachers also introduced **anti-Semitic** elements into their appeals. When the non-combatant crusaders set off earlier than the official departure date of August 1096, they were poorly provisioned. As a result, they pillaged lands on their way through Germany, often attacking wealthy Jewish communities who of course were non-Christian and thus were seen as 'infidels' on a par with the Muslims occupying Jerusalem. One of these crusading groups massacred the Jews of Speyer, Mainz, Trier and Cologne, twisting the Pope's call to kill the infidel to mean killing the Jews, and of course then seizing the wealth of their victims. Many thousands of Jews were either slaughtered or committed suicide to avoid forced conversion in the towns of Worms, Mainz and Prague. This was not part of Pope Urban's aim at all; Jews were supposed to be under the protection of the Church, which forbade forced conversion.

Sources

H The Chronicle of Solomon bar Simon, c.1140, describes the attacks on the Jews in Worms (Germany) in 1096–97:

They attacked the community of Worms. Those who remained in their homes were set upon by the steppe-wolves who pillaged men, women and infants, children and old people. They pulled down the stairways and destroyed the houses, looting and plundering; and they took the Torah scroll, trampled it in the mud, and tore and burned it. The enemy devoured the children of Israel with open maw.

I Albert of Aix (12th century) writing of the Jews in Mainz, Germany:

The Jews of this city, knowing of the slaughter of their brethren, and that they themselves could not escape the hands of so many, fled in hope of safety to Bishop Rothard. They put an infinite treasure in his guard and trust, having much faith in his protection, because he was Bishop of the city. Then that excellent Bishop cautiously set aside the incredible amount of money received from them. He placed the Jews in the very spacious hall of his own house, that they might remain safe and sound in a very secure and strong place.

ACTIVITY
Enquiries

1   Read Source H. What does the author mean by the 'steppe-wolves'?

2   Why did they trample the Torah scroll into the mud?

3   Compare Sources H and I as evidence for the attacks on the Jews. Where do they agree or differ in their authorship and content?

What happened to the People's Crusade?

The main problem was feeding the thousands of unauthorised pilgrims as they rampaged through Germany and Hungary on their way to Constantinople. Many thousands of Christians were also killed as they rioted over food shortages. The People's Crusade, as it has become known, was transported to Asia Minor by the Byzantine Emperor Alexius in August 1096 – no doubt he was keen to send them on their way as quickly as possible. In October the remaining pilgrims were wiped out near Nicaea (modern Iznik). Peter the Hermit survived and returned to Constantinople to await the official, military crusade.

Sources

(J) **Anna Comnena, describes the massacre of the People's Crusade:**

... when the mention of plunder and riches was heard, they straightway set out in tumult on the road which leads to Nicaea, forgetful of their military training and of observing discipline in going out to battle. For the Latins [westerners] are not only most fond of riches, as we said above, but when they give themselves to raiding any region for plunder, are also no longer obedient to reason, or any other check. Accordingly, since they were neither keeping order nor forming into lines, they fell into the ambush of the Turks around Draco and were wretchedly cut to pieces. Indeed, so great a multitude of Gauls [French] and Normans were cut down by the Ishmaelite sword that when the dead bodies of the killed, which were lying all about in the place, were brought together, they made a very great mound, or hill, or lookout place, lofty as a mountain ...

Anna Comnena, *The Alexiad*, Book 10

(K) **Raymond of Aguilers, writing around 1100, was in the Provençal army of Raymond of Toulouse, and was an eyewitness:**

We recognised, then, that the Emperor had betrayed Peter the Hermit, who had long before come to Constantinople with a great multitude. For he compelled him, ignorant of the locality and of all military matters, to cross the Strait with his men and exposed them to the Turks. Moreover, when the Turks from Nicea saw that unwarlike multitude, they cut them down without effort and delay to the number of sixty thousand.

ACTIVITY

Enquiries

1   Why, according to Anna Comnena in Source J, did the People's Crusade set out for Nicaea?

2   Compare sources J and K as evidence for the failure of the People's Crusade.

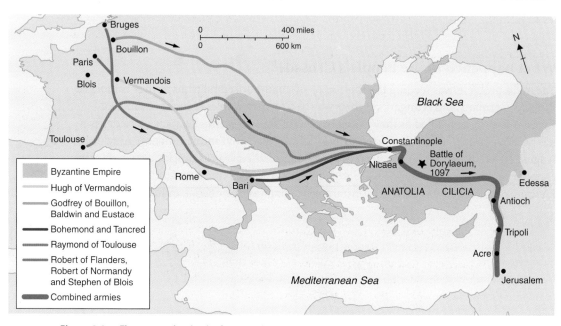

Figure 3.2   The routes taken by the first crusaders, 1096–99.

What was the response of Emperor Alexius to the main crusade?

The crusaders moved across Europe in regional contingents, with the intention of assembling at Constantinople. When he learnt of the thousands of people on their way to Constantinople, Emperor Alexius was not exactly overjoyed, especially since most of them were peasants in need of food. This was not what he had asked Pope Urban to send him.

The arrival of the People's Crusade was not an encouraging prospect, and the news that the deadly enemy of Byzantium, Bohemond of Taranto, was one of its leaders, filled the Greeks with apprehension. Bohemond had, after all, spent many years at war with the Greeks. Alexius had only asked Pope Urban to send a few thousand knights to join the Byzantine forces in the combat zone of Asia Minor. He had expected things to follow the usual pattern: he would pay them and they would retain their individual leaders and national identity, as had happened often in the past.

What were the cultural differences of the crusader army?

The armies of the great western European nobles arrived at Constantinople in late 1096 to early 1097. They were barely friendly towards one another, let alone the Byzantines. They had been recruited by, and remained with, their local and regional feudal lords. Differences in the dozens of languages and dialects across France, Flanders and Germany led to tensions and even though the papal legate, Adhemar of Le Puy, was technically the overall leader, it was virtually impossible for him to handle all the internal disputes.

Emperor Alexius was understandably concerned that this rabble would turn on his own great city, and he treated the tens of thousands of crusaders as potentially dangerous from the very beginning. It was, in a sense, an invasion by barbarians from the West. The crude, illiterate warriors from the damp, muddy hovels and basic stone fortresses of western Europe were overawed by the glittering spires and palaces of the Greek capital, and there was a real fear within the imperial city that the western barbarians would attack Constantinople. Alexius immediately posted coastguards to intercept lone ships straying away from the western fleet and suspended delivery of food supplies whenever the crusaders' behaviour grew violent. This only increased tension between East and West, and made the crusaders more likely to attack the city.

Source

(L) **Procopius, writing AD 490–560, describes the great church of Hagia Sophia in Constantinople, which was built by Emperor Justinian in 537:**

[The Church] is distinguished by indescribable beauty, excelling both in its size, and in the harmony of its measures, having no part excessive and none deficient; being more magnificent than ordinary buildings, and much more elegant than those which are not of so just a proportion. The church is singularly full of light and sunshine; you would declare that the place is not lighted by the sun from without, but that the rays are produced within itself, such an abundance of light is poured into this church. ... Moreover it is impossible accurately to describe the gold, and silver, and gems, presented by the Emperor Justinian, but by the description of one part, I leave the rest to be inferred. That part of the church which is especially sacred, and where the priests alone are allowed to enter, which is called the Sanctuary, contains forty thousand pounds' weight of silver.

Figure 3.3   Hagia Sophia, Istanbul (formerly Constantinople).

Did the crusaders swear an oath of loyalty to Emperor Alexius?

Alexius had no formal alliance with Pope Urban II. Adhemar, the papal legate, did not have the authority to impose a widespread uniform front on the many factions of baronial groups that made up the crusading army. Instead, Alexius decided to appeal to the western code of feudal honour and make the leaders his **vassals**. This would conform to their feudal customs of overlords and warrior loyalty, and would make them subject to his overall leadership. Count Hugh, brother of the King of France, agreed to this, probably because he was under virtual house-arrest after his disastrous shipwreck. Others were not so keen to swear the oath. When Duke Godfrey refused, Alexius limited the supplies to Godfrey's army, but he had to resume normal supplies when Godfrey's troops threatened violence. After several skirmishes on the outskirts of the city, Godfrey submitted. He knelt before Alexius and took the oath, promising to hand over any towns they captured to Alexius. Alexius announced that he was adopting Godfrey as his son, giving him gifts and paying his army.

Bohemond took the oath immediately, but he had his own agenda, according to Anna Comnena, the Emperor's historian daughter. Bohemond asked to be appointed *domestikos*, or commander, of the Byzantine army in the East: this would have made him leader of the

vassal

A vassal was subject to an overlord within the feudal structure that governed medieval society. He could be a landless peasant owing allegiance and farm-labouring duties to the local lord of the manor, or he could be a mighty prince swearing allegiance to an emperor to whom he owed military service. The greater the vassal, the more knights he usually provided to his lord.

crusade. Bohemond was already planning ahead and thinking about carving out his own principality in the East, after his failed raids on the Greek coast in previous decades.

> ## Source
>
> **From Anna Comnena's account**
>
> *The Emperor invited some of the Counts with Godfrey in order to advise them to suggest to Godfrey to take the oath; and as time was wasted owing to the long-winded talkativeness of the Latins, a false rumour reached the others that the Counts had been thrown into prison by the Emperor. Immediately numerous regiments moved on Byzantium, and to begin with they demolished the palace near the so-called Silver Lake. They also made an attack on the walls of Byzantium, not with siege-engines indeed, as they had none, but trusting to their numbers they actually had the impudence to try to set fire to the gate below the palace which is close to the chapel built long ago by one of the Emperors to the memory of Nicolas, the greatest saint in the hierarchy.*
>
> Anna Comnena, *The Alexiad* (Book 10), written around 1100

Count Raymond of Toulouse refused to swear the oath. He was the vassal of the King of France and was on the pilgrimage to serve the Lord, not an earthly prince. He was technically correct: feudal law did not allow someone to be the vassal of more than one lord. However, like all the others, Raymond was dependent on the Emperor for food and supplies. He agreed not to become Alexius' vassal, but swore not to attack the body or honour of his lord. Alexius was less generous to Raymond than to the others. Count Robert of Flanders, Duke Robert of Normandy and Count Stephen of Blois all swore to become vassals of Alexius, and were given treasures.

As far as Alexius was concerned, the crusaders had sworn to fight for him and to return to his empire the lands he had lost. These extended way beyond Asia Minor, to Syria, Palestine, Egypt and Mesopotamia. They also included Jerusalem, and the crusaders' oaths meant that if they freed the Holy Sepulchre from the Islamic world, then they would have to return it to the Byzantine emperor. As far as the evidence suggests, this was not the intention of Pope Urban II. The dealings between Alexius and the crusade leaders illustrate the distrust between East and West, and if this had been solved by the oath-takings, it was only a temporary pause in the deterioration of East–West relations.

> ## Source
>
> **From Anna Comnena's account**
>
> *When the Franks had all come together and had taken an oath to the emperor, there was one count who had the boldness to sit down upon the throne. The emperor, well knowing the pride of the Latins, kept silent, but Baldwin approached the Frankish count and taking him by the hand said, 'You ought not to sit there; that is an honour which the emperor permits to no one. Now that you are in this country, why do you not observe its customs?'*
>
> Anna Comnena, *The Alexiad* (Book 10), written around 1100

ACTIVITY

Period Studies

Why was there such distrust between the western crusaders and the Byzantines? To what extent were the motives of the crusaders misinterpreted by the Byzantines?

ACTIVITY

Enquiries

1 How does Source M demonstrate the level of distrust between the Latins and the Greeks in 1096?

2 Read Source N. What does it tell you of the attitudes of at least this one crusader towards the Byzantines?

Conclusion

The overarching motive for the crusaders was the promise of spiritual reward, not adventure or plunder. That said, the, different social classes had different intentions in fulfilling their vows. The mass of peasant–pilgrims wanted to get to Jerusalem, but many of them were diverted into attacking the Jews of Europe and many others died at Nicaea when the People's Crusade fizzled out. The nobles and princes of Europe were unavoidably bound up in the politics of the Byzantine Empire and were distrusted by the Greeks, a fact illustrated by the confusion over swearing the oath to Alexius. Many of the knights of western Europe undoubtedly hoped to gain land and riches after the example of the Norman conquests of England, southern Italy and Sicily, all in the name of God.

Whatever their varying motives, once the crusaders continued on from Constantinople into the hostile badlands of Muslim-held Asia Minor, the only thing that came to matter to them was simple: survival.

Review questions

Enquiries

1 Make notes on the distrust between the crusaders and the Byzantines. How serious was this distrust? Could it have endangered the crusade?

2 Is it fair to say that the First Crusade was already tainted with greed by the time it arrived at Constantinople and that the purity of Urban's message at Clermont had been cynically abused?

  Draw up a table of arguments for and against, then make a judgement and write it up into a paragraph.

Period Studies

3 Write an essay to answer the question: 'To what extent do you think the nobility of the First Crusade were motivated by religious passion or by hope of political and economic gain?'

Introduction

In the summer of 1097 the military crusade finally moved on from Constantinople. It took the 60,000 pilgrims two long years to pass through Anatolia (Turkey) before finally arriving at Jerusalem in July 1099. Two-thirds of the crusaders died on the way. Relations with the Byzantine Emperor Alexius grew worse, then broke down completely, because the crusaders' aim was not to support his war against the Turks but rather to capture Jerusalem. Relations between the crusaders deteriorated, with some of the leaders deserting or following their own agenda.

That said, the First Crusade was a resounding success for the following reasons:

- Weakness in the Islamic world allowed the crusader armies to gain victories in gradual stages.
- Early military support from the Byzantines.
- The crusaders were exploiting the Muslim tribal divisions and forming alliances as they progressed towards Jerusalem.
- The unprecedented religious zeal that Pope Urban had summoned at Clermont swept the crusaders through deserts, sieges and diseases to achieve the impossible.
- When they finally captured Jerusalem, the crusaders embarked on a wholesale slaughter of the inhabitants – Christians, Jews and Muslims.

Urban, however, died before the capture of Jerusalem, and his legate and leader of the crusade, Adhemar, had died on the journey. The crusade was no longer in the hands of the papacy and Emperor Alexius gained nothing. Never again was such passionate spiritualism seen on such a scale in Europe, and never again was a crusade so overwhelmingly successful.

Chapter timeline

November 1095	Pope Urban II preaches the crusade.
1096	The crusader armies set out from Europe.
1097	The armies depart from Constantinople, crossing the Straits of the Bosphorus to Asia Minor; Battle of Dorylaeum (June).
1097–98	Siege and capture of Antioch.
July 1099	Capture of Jerusalem.

KEY ISSUES

■ To what extent was the Muslim world prepared for the crusaders?

■ How did the crusaders gain their first victories?

■ How significant was the victory at Antioch?

■ Why did relations with Byzantium break down?

■ Did the papacy lose control of the crusade?

■ What happened at Jerusalem in 1099?

To what extent was the Muslim world prepared for the crusaders?

In brief, the Arab world was not at all prepared for the unprecedented onslaught it faced from the Christian West in 1095–99. This was very much to the crusaders' advantage. Even though the Turks had defeated the Byzantines at Manzikert in 1071 and had captured Antioch in 1084, the Islamic world was in a state of disarray at the time of the First Crusade. At the end of the eleventh century, in contrast to the world of western European monarchy, the Arab world was divided among rival Turkish **amirs** and Seljuk **atabegs**, the Fatimids in Egypt had a tenuous control of Palestine and the Abbasid caliph ruled in Baghdad only under the supervision of the Turkish sultan.

amirs, atabegs
Titles of the local Turkish chieftains and rulers.

Sources

(A) **William of Tyre, writing in the 1180s, describes the lack of Muslim unity:**

In former times almost every city had its own ruler, not dependent on one another ... who feared their own allies not less than the Christians and could not or would not readily unite to repulse the common danger or arm themselves for our destruction.

(B) **From T. Asbridge, *The First Crusade: a new history***

Had the Muslims of the Near East united in the face of the First Crusade it could not possibly have prevailed. The combined forces of Damascus, Aleppo and Mosul would surely have crushed the Franks outside the walls of Antioch; facing the collective might of the Abbasid and Fatimid caliphates, the Latins could never have mounted the sacred walls of Jerusalem. In the years to come, hundreds of thousands of Franks sought to equal the achievements of these First Crusaders, but in the face of burgeoning Islamic solidarity, none prospered.

Asbridge, T. (2005). *The First Crusade: a new history.* Simon and Schuster, UK.

ACTIVITY

Enquiries

Compare Sources A and B as evidence for the lack of Muslim unity.

Sunni and Shia

The basic division in the Islamic faith, still current today, was between the Sunni and the Shia. This split went back to the death of the prophet Muhammad (AD 632), when one group recognised Ali, Muhammad's cousin and son-in-law, as the next caliph, that is, the prophet's representative. This group is known as the Shia, *Shi'atu Ali* meaning 'Ali's group'. However, another group recognised Abu Bakr, one of Muhammad's closest associates, as caliph. By the 1070s, the Sunni controlled Asia Minor and Syria, under the leadership of the caliph of Baghdad, while the Shia ruled Egypt under a caliph based in Cairo. These two groups hated each other more than they hated the newly arrived Christian crusaders, and often formed alliances with the crusaders to make gains on their fellow-Muslim enemy.

A power vacuum in Anatolia

After the death of the great Seljuk Sultan Malik Shah in 1092, several caliphs and **viziers** from both the Sunni and the Shia branches of Islam died in 1094. This left a power vacuum in Anatolia at the very time the Christian West was preparing to launch the First Crusade. When the first crusaders arrived, they found a series of petty rulers fighting for leadership of the region. These leaders seemed unaware that the Christians had come not just to retake former Byzantine territory in Asia Minor but to march all the way to Jerusalem and create a new kingdom there. The Sunni caliph in Baghdad did not get involved, but had there been a coherent and strong Muslim army under another Malik Shah, the crusader army would probably not have got through.

vizier

In some Muslim countries, a high-ranking government official, the chief counsellor to a caliph.

The Muslim weaknesses also led the Byzantines to believe that they could realistically recover many of their lost lands in Asia Minor and Syria. In this light, the crusade leaders' oaths of loyalty to Alexius have real meaning when the crusaders began to win their first victories.

Figure 4.1 Anatolia (Turkey) during the First Crusade, showing the sites of the battles of Manzikert, Nicaea and Dorylaeum.

How did the crusaders gain their first victories?

After settling their differences with Alexius, the main crusader army crossed the Straits of the Bosphorus into Asia Minor in May 1097. With Byzantine forces, they then captured the town of Nicaea, the capital of the Seljuk ruler Kilij Arslan. It was essential to capture this town, in order to gain access to the main land route through Asia Minor to Syria. The Turks negotiated with Emperor Alexius, who was there in person, and surrendered to him to avoid a massacre. The town was therefore officially captured by the Emperor, who distributed plunder to the crusaders to keep them happy. Alexius gathered the leaders and all but Raymond swore loyalty to the Emperor, who now delegated command of his troops to a general named Taticius. The Emperor himself would supply troops and food, and would follow the crusaders as they approached Jerusalem.

The Battle of Dorylaeum

In June 1097 the crusade army resumed its journey across Asia Minor, and soon met an army despatched by Sultan Kilij Arslan on the plain of Dorylaeum (see Figure 4.1). Bohemond's army was attacked first and was driven back by the rapid archery fire of the Turks. However, with assistance from Godfrey they counter-attacked, and when the other crusade contingents came in on the flanks of the Turkish forces, the Turks fled. Lessons were learnt on both sides: the crusaders got their first experience of confronting lightly armed Turkish mounted archers who were able to wheel their mares back and forth in feigned retreats, and the Turks came face to face with the fearsome heavy cavalry charge of the western armed knights. It was a great victory for the crusaders and opened the way through to the heart of Asia Minor, which they crossed in the full heat of the summer, losing many horses on the way.

Source

C The anonymous author of the *Deeds of the Franks*, writing around 1100, describes the Battle of Dorylaeum:

Our forces were drawn up in one continuous battle line. The Bishop of Le Puy approached by way of another mountain and thus the unbelieving Turks were surrounded on all sides. Raymond of St-Gilles also fought on the left side. On the right there were Duke Godfrey, the Count of Flanders (a most valiant knight), and Hugh of France, together with many others whose names I know not. As soon as our knights arrived, the Turks, Arabs, Saracens and all the barbarian tribes speedily took flight through the byways of the mountains and plains. With extraordinary speed they fled to their tents but were unable to remain there long. Again they took flight and we followed, killing them as we went, for a whole day …

ACTIVITY
Enquiries

What can we learn about the Battle of Dorylaeum from Source C? How useful is its content?

Why was Edessa important?

After the Battle of Dorylaeum, Baldwin of Boulogne headed east towards the city of **Edessa**, which was under the rule of the Christian **Armenians**. Baldwin was adopted as the heir to the county and by the spring of 1098 he had established the first of the Latin settlements which was to last 46 years. The region was fertile and prosperous, and supplied food and resources for the other Christian areas further south, which were less fertile. The city was captured by the Muslims in 1144 (see pages 82–83), the first of the crusader states to fall.

Edessa

Now the modern Turkish town of Sanli Urfa, this is perhaps the oldest continually inhabited city on earth, dating from the eighth century BC. Under the Byzantines it was a powerful political and ecclesiastical centre, with schools and monasteries.

Armenians

The kingdom of Armenia was founded in the sixth century BC. In the very early fourth century AD, it became the first state to adopt Christianity. The kingdom was taken over by the Byzantine Empire and the Armenians found themselves increasingly squeezed by the Seljuk Turks. The Armenians saw the arrival of Baldwin as a welcome relief from the domination of both Turks and Byzantines.

How significant was the victory at Antioch?

While Baldwin of Boulogne was building his new crusader state at Edessa, the main crusader army had marched south. By October 1097 they had arrived at the Muslim-held city of Antioch in northern Syria. Antioch was an important Christian city because it was the home of the apostle Luke, the author of one of the Christian gospels. It was also one of the five Christian cities that had a **patriarch**. Antioch was also a massive walled citadel, heavily defended and in no mood to surrender without a fight to the crusaders. It was built on hills surrounded by 400 towers. The siege and eventual capture of Antioch was to be the hardest time for the crusade army and would involve all of them; it would also end the co-operation between the crusaders and the Byzantines.

patriarch

A senior Christian bishop in one of the most ancient cities (Rome, Constantinople, Alexandria, Antioch and Jerusalem).

The siege of Antioch

The siege began in 1097 and was to last for eight months through the long and bitter winter. It was impossible for the crusaders to encircle the city's 25 miles of walls to prevent food supplies from coming in, so it was the besieging crusaders who starved. They lost most of their horses and suffered from outbreaks of disease. In October the crusaders seized control of the tower commanding entry to the bridge over the River Orontes and the Gate of St Paul. Ships sent by Guy of Boulogne and the **Genoese** secured a coastal supply line from the Byzantine ports in Asia Minor. However, this was not enough and famine developed in the crusader army. People began to desert, including Peter the Hermit, who was discovered and publicly admonished by Bohemond.

Geneoese

Genoa was a city-state in northern Italy. It grew wealthy on maritime trade and had a powerful navy.

Figure 4.3   A thirteenth-century manuscript depicting siege warfare along the lines of biological warfare, as severed heads are catapulted into enemy positions to spread disease.

What was the role of Bohemond?

At this critical point, in January 1098 the leader of the Byzantine army, Alexius' general, Taticius, left the siege. His troops remained under the command of Bohemond, who may have persuaded Taticius that his life was in danger. The following months saw various setbacks and advances, but no great breakthrough in the siege. By now the sultan had despatched a large relief force to come to the aid of the citizens of Antioch. Baldwin delayed these troops at Edessa for some weeks, giving the crusaders vital breathing space. It was Bohemond, however, who devised a cunning plan to have the city betrayed to the crusaders. He enlisted the help of an Armenian named Firouz, who was keeper of the Tower of the Two Sisters, and on the night of 2 June a rope was lowered from the walls of the city. The crusaders gained entry, and slaughtered everyone they could find and seized much plunder. Bohemond raised his flag on the walls of the tower.

Source

D Raymond of Aguilers, writing around 1100, describes the crusaders' capture of Antioch:

Accordingly, when the plan had been communicated, the princes sent Bohemund and the Duke of Lorraine and the Count of Flanders to try it out. And when they had come to the hill of the city at midnight, an intermediary sent back by him who was surrendering the city said, 'Wait until the light passes.' For three or four men went along the walls of the city with lamps all night, rousing and admonishing the watchers. After this, however, our men approached the wall, raised a ladder, and began to ascend it. And when the day whitened, our standards appeared on the southern hill of the city. When the disturbed citizens saw our men on the mountain above them, some fled through the gate, others hurled themselves headlong. No one resisted; in truth, the Lord had confounded them.

E This extract from *The Deeds of the Franks*, written by an anonymous author around 1100, describes attacks on Nicaea, which was captured before Antioch:

... we began to attack the city on all sides, and to construct machines of wood, and wooden towers, with which we might be able to destroy towers on the walls. We attacked the city so bravely and so fiercely that we even undermined its wall ... moreover, our men hurled the heads of the killed far into the city, that they [the Turks] might be the more terrified thereat. Then the Count of St Gilles and the Bishop of Puy took counsel together as to how they might have undermined a certain tower which was opposite their tents. Men were assigned to do the digging, with arbalistae [crossbows] and bowmen to defend them on all sides. So they dug to the foundations of the wall and fixed timbers and wood under it and then set fire to it. However, evening had come; the tower had already fallen in the night, and because it was night they could not fight with the enemy. Indeed, during that night the Turks hastily built up and restored the wall so strongly that when day came no one could harm them on that side.

ACTIVITY

Enquiries

Compare Sources D and E as evidence for crusade siege warfare.

ACTIVITY

Period Studies

Look at the methods of crusading warfare used in the early campaigns of the First Crusade.

Assess the success of these various methods.

- Giving battle, using cavalry, infantry and archery.
- Besieging castles and towns.
- Cutting off food supplies.
- Infiltrating the walls by stealth or at night and undermining the walls by tunnelling.
- Full-frontal assaults, using ladders and bombardments.

The next problem was was that the defenders retreated to Antioch's main citadel and an outside relief force of Muslims led by **Kerbogha** arrived from Mosul on 4 June. The crusaders became trapped between the two. With Kerbogha were the King of Damascus, the Emir of Homs and many leaders from Iraq. Things were now very bad for the crusaders, and they were made worse by deserters, including Duke Robert of Normandy who withdrew to Latakia (on the Syrian coast) and Stephen of Blois, who told the Emperor Alexius on his return journey that the crusade was finished. As a result, the Greek reinforcements accompanied by Emperor Alexius turned back to Constantinople. Starvation was the biggest killer: on 12 June Bohemond and Adhemar had to close the gates of the crusader camp to prevent their own army breaking out and fleeing.

> **BIOGRAPHY**
>
> **Kerbogha**
>
> Kerbogha was the atabeg of Mosul. He supported the Sultan of Baghdad, and was seen by the crusaders as their most feared opponent, the leader of a vast army of Turks, Arabs, Saracens, Kurds and Persians. He was not in fact the official leader of the Arab world, but rather a merciless and brutal regional warlord who bullied, intimidated and murdered his way into forging the tribes of northern Syria into his alliance against the crusaders.

Holy Lance

The lance that pierced the side of Christ during the crucifixion.

ordeal by fire

In medieval times, a person's innocence was often tested by subjecting them to ordeals such as walking through fire or being submerged in water. If they survived, this was taken as God's proof of their innocence.

The Miracle of the Holy Lance

Something urgent was needed: a miracle. A pilgrim named Peter Bartholomew claimed to have had a vision where St Andrew revealed to him the whereabouts of the **Holy Lance**. Whoever found the lance would triumph in battle. Peter excavated under the church of St Peter in Antioch and found the lance on 14 June (some crusaders doubted its authenticity and Peter died in the **ordeal by fire**, trying to prove it was authentic). But the Lance, real or not, gave most of the crusaders such new hope that they sent out a delegation to Kerbogha, asking him to withdraw. When he refused, the crusader army formed into battle groups led by Bohemond – now the crusaders' supreme commander, as Count Raymond was ill. They forced the invading Muslim army to flee. The Muslim defenders inside the citadel then surrendered and Bohemond's flag was raised on the walls of the citadel.

Sources

(F) **From the *Deeds of the Franks* (Anonymous), written around 1100:**

So terrible was the famine that men boiled and ate the leaves of figs, vines, thistles and all kinds of trees. Others stewed the dried skins of horses, camels, asses, oxen or buffaloes, which they ate.

(G) **Raymond of Aguilers describes the discovery of the Holy Lance:**

And after we had dug from morning to evening, some began to despair of finding the Lance. The youth who had spoken of the Lance, however, upon seeing us worn out, disrobed and, taking off his shoes, descended into the pit in his shirt, earnestly entreating us to pray to God give us His Lance for the comfort and victory of His people. At length, the Lord was minded through the grace of His mercy to show us His Lance. And I, who have written this, kissed it when the point alone had as yet appeared above ground. What great joy and exultation then filled the city I cannot describe.

Why did relations with Byzantium break down?

The successes of the crusaders in Asia Minor meant that Emperor Alexius was now in a position to regain many of his former possessions. The Aegean coastline and the region inland to Cappadocia were his, as per the agreement made with the crusaders. Alexius was personally on his way with an army to help the crusaders at Antioch in May 1098 when he encountered the deserter, Stephen of Blois. Stephen convinced him that the crusaders were finished, crushed between the defending Muslims in the citadel and the relief force sent by the Sultan. On hearing this news, Alexius ordered his troops to withdraw and turned back towards Constantinople.

News of the Emperor's retreat may well have encouraged Bohemond to plan his own conquest of Antioch, but even after the city's capture the crusade leaders sent messengers to Alexius, inviting him to take possession of the town and join them for the march on Jerusalem. It was clear in most of the barons' minds that their oaths to Alexius were still binding.

Alexius received the invitation, but he did not reply until the spring of 1099. He decided not to go south, probably because of the difficulties of the journey: it was too risky and too costly. In any case, Alexius was not interested in Jerusalem and he had been negotiating with the Egyptians.

Sources

(H) **From a letter from Emperor Alexius to the Abbot of Monte Cassino (1098):**

I beseech you earnestly to furnish aid to the army of Franks, your most thoughtful letters state. Let your Venerable Holiness be assured on that score, for my empire has been spread over them and will aid and advise them on all matters; indeed, it has already cooperated with them according to its ability, not as a friend, or relative, but like a father. It has expended among them more than anyone can enumerate. And had not my empire so cooperated with them and aided them, who else would have afforded them help?

(I) **This passage from *The Deeds of the Franks*, written around 1100 by an anonymous crusader eyewitness, describes the desertion of the Byzantine military commander, Taticius, who promises to bring supplies but never returns:**

Meanwhile the hostile Taticius, upon hearing that the army of the Turks had come upon us, said that he was afraid, thinking that we would all perish and fall into the hands of the enemy. Fabricating all the falsehoods which he could industriously scatter, he said: 'Seignors and most illustrious men, you see that we are here in the greatest need, and aid is coming to us from no side. So permit me now to return to my country of Romania [Byzantium], and I will, for certain, cause many ships to come hither by sea, laden with grain, wine, barley, meat, butter, and cheese, and all the goods which you need. I shall also cause horses to be brought for sale, and a market to be brought hither in the fealty of the Emperor.'

The Egyptian negotiations

It was not only Alexius who was talking to the Egyptians. During the siege of Antioch, Count Raymond had sent a letter to the vizier al-Afdal and this included a promise by the Egyptian **Fatimids** to hand over free Jerusalem if the crusaders allied with the Fatimid attack against the Seljuks, their deadly enemies. Letters captured from the Fatimids then revealed that they were also negotiating with Alexius, and that he had urged them not to keep their promises to the crusaders. The crusaders saw this as the worst kind of treachery: they had sworn an oath of loyalty to Alexius and he had promised to be their overlord and protect them, not betray them to the infidel. Most vehement in his anger was Bohemond, a former enemy of the Emperor and a fierce supporter of the oath, and now master of Antioch. He had done most to take the citadel of Antioch on the assumption that the Emperor would grant him a large Byzantine fief as a reward. But Bohemond must have known that he was risking a great deal and after the departure of Taticius, he probably began thinking about seizing territory for himself.

Fatimids

The Fatimid caliphate was founded in Egypt in 909, and was based in Cairo from 973, as a rival to the Abbasid caliphate in Baghdad. It was dependent on the army. After 1094 it lost support of the extremist Ismailites and was severely weakened as a political and military force, hence its negotiations with the Byzantines and the crusaders.

Did the papacy lose control of the crusade?

The crusaders sent their letter to Alexius on 3 July 1098. While waiting in the summer heat for his reply and for reinforcements, the papal legate, Bishop Adhemar of Le Puy, was struck down by epidemic. No other churchman had the authority of Adhemar, and his death weakened the unity of the crusade leadership. In September the barons wrote to Pope Urban, begging him to come and lead them to Jerusalem. In Italy, Urban declared that he would indeed leave for the Holy Land, but he never did so.

> **Source**
>
> **(J)** **An extract from a letter from the crusaders to Pope Urban, 11 September 1098:**
>
> *We beg you then, holy father, come among your children … come and lead us in the path that you have mapped out and open for us the gates of the one and only Jerusalem, come and liberate with us the tomb of Jesus Christ and make the name of Christian prevail over all other names.*

ACTIVITY

Enquiries

Read Source J. Why do you think the crusaders felt that they needed the Pope to lead them into Jerusalem?

The beginnings of a 'Latin East'

The crusade stalled in the autumn of 1098, waiting to hear from the Emperor and the Pope. As time passed, it was clear that the crusaders would not, after all, be handing over their gains.

And so they started to carve out territories for themselves. In Antioch, Count Raymond held on to several fortresses, refusing to give them to Bohemond, who was creating his principality around Antioch. In Edessa, Baldwin was creating a Franco-Armenian principality. Raymond installed one of his clerics, Peter of Narbonne, as Bishop of Albara, thus bypassing papal and imperial authority. It looked increasingly as though the influence of the Pope in Rome was diminishing rapidly.

What happened at Jerusalem in 1099?

It was clear that the leadership of the main army was by no means united after the taking of Edessa and Antioch. Now that it was understood that the Emperor would not be joining the army and Adhemar's death had removed direct papal influence, it was the religious devotion of the thousands of surviving pilgrims which drove the crusade towards Jerusalem, the final destination. The great mass of knights, pilgrims and clergy grew tired of waiting for the great lords to decide who had what towns and fortresses in the area. They now forced Raymond of Toulouse to assume leadership of the crusade, first having destroyed the town of Ma'arrat, which had recently been captured by Raymond's troops.

The march on Jerusalem

There were probably around 25,000 crusaders who embarked on the final march to Jerusalem. Many thousands had died either in battle or from disease and sickness, and many had deserted. Those who remained were battle-hardened and experienced in the ways of the eastern terrain and warfare. They marched in various contingents led by Raymond of Toulouse, Robert of Flanders and Godfrey of Bouillon. The march on Jerusalem was simplified by the fragmented nature of the local Arab communities, who were virtually independent of one another. No help was offered from the Fatimids in Egypt. Indeed, the emirs of Shaizar, Homs and Tripoli actually gave the crusaders money and gifts to to stay away from their towns and leave them in peace. The towns of Beirut, Sidon, Tyre and Caesarea all paid ransoms to avoid capture, supplying the crusaders with all they needed. In May, letters arrived from the Emperor Alexius, complaining about Bohemond's behaviour and asking the crusaders to wait for Alexius to join them. The crusaders, apart from Raymond, refused to wait and marched on, with the Christian fleet shadowing them along the coast.

The siege of Jerusalem

The increasing confidence that the crusaders were carving out their own Christian kingdom independent from the Byzantine Emperor and free from papal intervention was reflected in the installation of the new bishop at Ramla, at the church of St George at Lydda on 3 June. On 7 June they occupied Bethlehem and then massed before Jerusalem, three years after leaving Europe.

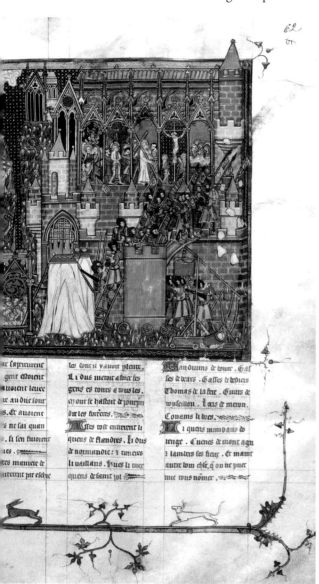

Jerusalem was controlled by Egyptian Fatimid forces, led by Iftikhar ad-Dawla, who had poisoned the wells and expelled the Christians from the strongly garrisoned city. An attack on 13 June failed due to a shortage of ladders with which to scale the city walls, but when two Genoese ships arrived at Jaffa with timber to construct siege machines, things looked up; towers and catapults were built and from now on, the offensive would be an organised one.

In the full heat of midsummer, the crusaders fasted on 8 July and walked barefoot to the Mount of Olives, praying for God's aid. The decision was taken to attack the eastern part of the city walls. On 15 July, Godfrey of Bouillon's men crossed the ramparts with a rolling tower and entered the city. Ladders enabled the other attackers to get in and the city was taken.

Siege of Jerusalem, from a thirteenth-century manuscript.

The massacre of the defenders

The crusaders had taken heavy casualties during the attack. Now that they were inside the city, they slaughtered thousands – Muslims, Jews, Christians, men, women and children. Thousands fled to the mighty al-Aqsa mosque, but were all killed; thousands of Jews in the Jewish Quarter were killed, with many burning to death inside the synagogues where they had taken refuge. But many hundreds of others were escorted to safety, including Iftikhar, who surrendered the citadel. The slaughter was indiscriminate and not systematic; hundreds of Muslims were later resettled in Damascus.

Source

(K) Fulcher of Chartres describes the crusaders' arrival in Jerusalem (c.1100):

... they joyfully rushed into the city to pursue and kill the nefarious enemies, as their comrades were already doing. A great fight took place in the court and porch of the temples, where they were unable to escape from our gladiators. Many fled to the roof of the temple of Solomon, and were shot with arrows, so that they fell to the ground dead. In this temple almost ten thousand were killed. Indeed, if you had been there you would have seen our feet coloured to our ankles with the blood of the slain. But what more shall I relate? None of them were left alive; neither women nor children were spared.

(L) William of Tyre, writing around the 1180s, describes the slaughter:

Everywhere lay fragments of human bodies, and the very ground was covered with the blood of the slain. Still more dreadful was it to gaze upon the victors themselves, dripping with blood from head to foot ... then, clad in fresh garments, with clean hands and bare feet, in humility they began to make the rounds of the venerable places which the Saviour had deigned to sanctify and make glorious with His bodily presence ... with particular veneration they approached the church of the passion and Resurrection of the Lord ...

ACTIVITY

Enquiries

Compare Sources K and L as evidence for the slaughter of the inhabitants of Jerusalem in July 1099.

The non-combatant pilgrims found their way to the church of the Holy Sepulchre, the destination of the epic journey, to venerate the tomb of Christ and give thanks for their safe arrival. They were later joined by the blood-soaked warriors.

How did the Muslims respond?

The counts of Flanders and Normandy were already on their way home when news arrived of vizier al-Afdal's approaching army at Ascalon; Godfrey got word to them and they joined with Raymond to surprise the Muslim army and drive them into the sea, seizing much plunder. For the time being, the threat from Egypt was neutralised. Around 20,000 crusaders, led by the counts of Flanders, Normandy and Toulouse, marched north on their way home, travelling by ship to Constantinople to be welcomed with honour by the Emperor.

The threat from the Muslim world in general never materialised; the Seljuk sultan was dealing with events in Persia and did not bring an army to confront the westerners. The First Crusade was over.

Conclusion: why was the First Crusade so successful?

The First Crusade was an unprecedented and unique success. Never again was a crusade so overwhelmingly victorious against the Muslim world; indeed most future crusades would fail to achieve significant defeats of the Arab armies.

It was successful for the following reasons, in order of priority:

- Muslim disunity and lack of a single leader to defeat the crusaders
- crusader military tactics in battles and sieges
- religious devotion and fervour
- support from Byzantium in the early stages.

What were the consequences of The First Crusade?

Successful though the crusade was in capturing Jerusalem, it was not altogether a success for the papacy, which lost direct control of the movement (Urban II was dead by the time news of the crusaders' conquest of Jerusalem reached Rome) and it was certainly not a success for the Byzantine Emperor Alexius. Furthermore, the crusade had revealed the many differences in the ambitions and desires of the nobles who were its leaders: they were by no means innocent Christians motivated solely by the rewards of the pilgrimage.

Figure 4.2: The Kingdom of Jerusalem and the crusader states of Edessa, Antioch and Tripoli after the First Crusade.

The consequences of the First Crusade were far-reaching and almost totally unforeseen:

■ The capture of Antioch was a significant turning point. The death of Adhemar of Le Puy, papal legate and official leader of the crusade, effectively removed the crusade from papal hands. Secondly, divisions among the crusade's leadership became apparent during the siege. Stephen of Blois' desertion was perfidious, but after Alexius' retreat to Constantinople, some of the crusaders said that the oaths of loyalty they had sworn to Alexius were now invalid. Bohemond of Taranto was especially keen to renege on his oath, because he had plans to keep Antioch after its capture, assuming the title Prince of Antioch. This led to poor relations between Constantinople and Antioch for decades. The ugly disputes between Raymond and Bohemond did nothing to endear them to the massed ranks of pilgrims who were eager to march on Jerusalem.

■ Once the crusaders were actually in the Holy Land, they became aware of the diversity of Muslim lordships and alliances. This made the papal view of cleansing the Christian churches of the 'infidel' seem too simplistic. Those crusaders who settled quickly realised that the only way to survive was to form alliances with the local Muslim factions, setting Seljuk against Fatimid, Aleppo against Damascus and so on.

■ After the capture of Jerusalem, the crusaders were in new territory. The higher authorities of pope and emperor were thousands of miles away. Those who had survived and those who remained behind now had to build a new kingdom to defend the Holy City.

Review questions

Plan your answers by creating two columns headed 'for' and 'against' in note form. Make a judgement before you begin writing, and distinguish clearly between the two sides of the argument.

1 To what extent did the lack of Muslim unity assist the crusaders in winning their victories?

2 How far was Bohemond merely a self-serving soldier of fortune?

3 To what extent had the crusade become a political movement dominated by faction and cynical manipulation by 1099?

5 How did the crusader kingdom develop and survive from 1100 to 1130?

Key Questions:

In this chapter you will learn:

- How the kingdom was created and expanded
- How the kingdom was governed
- Why the feudal customs of the West were important
- Why the lack of Muslim unity aided the survival of the kingdom

You will also develop the following skills:

- Assessing the language and tone of documents
- Comparing sources and their limitations
- Assessing the importance of kingship and the feudal system in the new kingdom
- Making a judgement on the crusaders' success and the Muslim weakness

Introduction

Soon after the capture of Jerusalem, most of the crusaders did what pilgrims normally do: they went home. The few thousand left behind were faced with the task of establishing a permanent Christian province. This became the kingdom of Jerusalem with its outlying counties, and was known in the West as Outremer ('the land over the sea'). The big names of the First Crusade – Baldwin, Godfrey, Bohemond and Raymond – were the men who founded these territories. They had already begun to establish them before the capture of Jerusalem. There was no longer any question of handing over land to the Emperor Alexius in Constantinople.

The kingdom developed in the following ways:

- A king was chosen to lead the new kingdom.
- More ports, cities and territories were captured in the period 1100–30.
- The outlying territories were formed into three provinces: the counties of Antioch, Edessa and Tripoli.
- The government of the kingdom and the provinces had their own legal and political structures, based on both Western and local traditions and customs.
- The king was the feudal overlord of the region in an attempt to replicate the feudal monarchies of the West (see Chapter 1).

The survival of the kingdom in the early decades was precarious and depended greatly on the lack of any conspicuous unity in the Muslim world. Crusader rulers formed alliances with various Muslim tribes and leaders when it suited them. Relations with the Byzantine Empire deteriorated to the point where the Emperor was actively seeking Muslim aid against the crusaders after being attacked again by Bohemond.

Chapter timeline

July 1099	Crusaders storm and capture Jerusalem. Godfrey of Bouillon becomes Advocate of the Holy Sepulchre.
1100	Baldwin I becomes King of Jerusalem.
1101	Capture of the port of Caesarea.
1102	New crusade helps the kingdom to survive.
1104	Capture of the port of Acre.
1108	Bohemond diverts another crusade to attack the Greeks.
1110	Capture of Beirut and Sidon.
1112	Death of Bohemond.
1118	Death of Baldwin I: accession of his cousin, Baldwin II.
1119	Battle of the Field of Blood; Roger of Antioch killed with his army.
1124	Capture of the port of Tyre.

KEY ISSUES

■ Who would be king?

■ What were the new conquests after Jerusalem?

■ What were the crusader states?

■ How was the crusader kingdom governed?

■ How significant was the lack of Muslim unity?

E

5 How did the crusader kingdom develop and survive from 1100 to 1130?

Who would be king?

The question of the leadership of the Holy City was raised immediately after its capture. At the council held on 17 July, the clergy argued that the city should be ruled by a patriarch and not a lay prince. Their problem was that no great churchman was present to take the post and instead the barons chose a secular leader to lead the defence of the city. The obvious choice was Raymond of Toulouse, who had been the most consistent leader from the start. However, Raymond had made enemies and many of his southern French followers were not remaining in the Holy Land. Raymond turned down the offer and the post was offered to Godfrey of Bouillon, who was supported by Robert of Normandy and Robert of Flanders. Godfrey refused the title of king, saying that he could not wear a crown of gold in the place where Christ had worn a crown of thorns (a reference to the crucifixion). Godfrey is thereafter referred to as 'duke' and 'advocate' of the Holy Sepulchre, but when he died childless in 1100, his brother Baldwin of Boulogne had no qualms about accepting the title and was crowned King of Jerusalem.

Source

(A) **Raymond of Aguilers, writing around 1100, describes the election of Godfrey:**

Accordingly, after six or seven days the princes solemnly began to consider the matter of choosing a ruler, who, assuming charge of all matters, should collect the tributes of the region, to whom the peasants of the land could turn, and who would see to it that the land was not further devastated. While this was taking place, some of the clergy assembled and said to the princes, 'We approve your election, but if you proceed rightly and properly, you will first choose a spiritual vicar, as eternal matters come before temporal; after this, a ruler to preside over secular matters. Otherwise, we shall hold invalid whatever you do.' The princes were exceedingly angered when they heard this and proceeded the more quickly with the election. The clergy had been weakened by the departure [i.e. death] of Lord Adhemar, Pontiff of Puy, who in his life had held our army together with holy deeds and words, like a second Moses. The princes, disregarding admonition and opposition, urged the Count of St Gilles [Raymond of Toulouse] to accept the kingdom. But he said that he abhorred the name of king in that city, though he would consent to have others accept it. For this reason they together chose the Duke [Godfrey of Bouillon] and placed him in charge of the Sepulchre of the Lord.

ACTIVITY
Enquiries

Read Source A.

1 What is meant by 'a spiritual vicar'?

2 How significant was the death of Adhemar?

3 Why do you think Raymond 'abhorred the name of king in that city'?

4 How useful is Source A for information on Godfrey's election?

The kings of Jerusalem 1100–31

Baldwin I of Jerusalem

Baldwin was a tall man and a great warrior who had already founded the County of Edessa. His reign (1100–18) was a successful one, Acre was taken in 1104, Beirut and Sidon in 1110 and in 1115 he built a castle at Montreal in Transjordan. This castle dominated the area east of the River Jordan and the Dead Sea, extending down to the Red Sea port of Eilat; it thus controlled the trade routes from Damascus to Egypt. Baldwin died in 1118, and was succeeded by his cousin, Baldwin II.

Baldwin II

Baldwin II was the count of Edessa, and ruled for thirteen years (1118–31). He too was a tall man and had a thin blond beard to his waist. He was both a great warrior and a holy man – he had calluses on his knees from constant kneeling in prayer. Baldwin II led nineteen campaigns during his reign, was held captive 1122–23, acted as regent in Antioch 1119–26 and governed it directly in 1130.

He spent most of his time in the saddle on campaign either near Egypt or Damascus, winning battles and coming close to taking Damascus. Baldwin encouraged the master of the new Templar Order (see pages 72–75), Hugh of Payns, to travel to the West to raise money and soldiers for what amounted to a new crusade against Damascus.

Baldwin had four daughters, and he managed to secure the succession when the eldest, Melisende, married the formidable Count Fulk of Anjou. Fulk brought with him hundreds of troops from Anjou to join the attack on Damascus. They remained with him after he became king in 1131 on Baldwin II's death.

What were the new conquests after Jerusalem?

The crusade of 1101

It was just as well for the crusaders that the Muslim world was too disunited to mount an organised counter-attack, because the Christian hold on the Holy Land was tenuous after the departure of the majority of the crusaders in 1100. Despite the absence of a unified Arab army, during the first decades of the kingdom the crusaders were beset with ceaseless campaigning in the form of marches, sieges and raids. In 1100 the new king of Jerusalem, Baldwin I, held just Jerusalem, Bethlehem and Jaffa, his only port. In May 1101 the crusaders captured the port of Caesarea. This was good for the crusaders, but it was not enough: Antioch, their other main base of strength, was 300 miles away. Therefore a new crusade was needed, and the appeal for aid summoned back many of those who had deserted the First Crusade (including Stephen of Blois, who had left during the siege of Antioch) and those who had not managed to join it. This crusade of 1101 reached the Holy Land in 1102. It had been much depleted by attacks during its journey through Asia Minor, and many more died (including Stephen) at the Battle of Ramla, but this new crusade helped the struggling kingdom to survive.

The crusade of 1108

The hero of the First Crusade, Bohemond, Prince of Antioch, returned to Europe in 1106 to great crowds of fans wanting to hear tales of his exploits. Bohemond set his sights high and married no less than the daughter of the King of France, Constance, and with the support of the new pope, Paschal II, launched a new crusade. Bohemond, however, was soon up to his old tricks, leading the army in 1107 not directly to Antioch but to the Byzantine port of Durazzo (modern Durrës in Albania). This attack on the Greeks seemed to have been sanctioned by the Pope, which signals a major development in the crusading ideal of holy war against the so-called infidel. Bohemond was not successful and had to become an imperial vassal of Emperor Alexius; part of his army continued to Jerusalem where again, they were needed.

Source

(B) The Muslim historian, Ibn al Qalinisi, in his *Continuation of the Chronicle of Damascus*, written 1140–60, describes the efforts of the Byzantine Emperor Alexius to get the Muslims to attack the crusaders in the period 1110–11. This extract illustrates the worsening relations between Byzantine Christians and the crusaders:

The envoy of the tyrant Emperor arrived at the court of Sultan Mohammed in Baghdad. The aim was an exhortation to attack the Franks and inflict great losses upon them, to unite to drive them out of their territories, and to do the utmost to exterminate them before they were too firmly established in their menacing position and their evil became uncontrollable. The Emperor had prevented the Franks from crossing his dominions to the lands of the Muslims and had gone to war with them. He wanted the Muslims to take concerted action to fight them and root the crusaders out of these lands.

ACTIVITY
Enquiries

Read Source B and answer the following questions.

1   Why did the Byzantine Emperor want the Muslims to take action against the crusaders?

2   How reliable is Source B regarding the Byzantine Emperor's apparent treachery? (Think about the origin of the source and possibly its purpose and nature.)

The Battle of the Field of Blood (1119)

Just over a year after becoming king of Jerusalem, Baldwin II faced a major threat from inside the Muslim world. On 28 June 1119, Roger of Antioch's army was surrounded to the west of Aleppo and the crusader army was wiped out. Almost all 700 knights and 3000 footsoldiers were killed or captured, and Roger was killed. King Baldwin had to march north and take control of Antioch, which had suffered raids. Baldwin restored order but the crusade resources had taken a big hit.

The 'crusade' of 1120 and the capture of Tyre (1124)

Part of the consequence of the Battle of the Field of Blood was a hardening of relations between East and West. A church council convened at Nablus early in 1120 forbade sexual relations between Christians and Muslims. The punishment for men was castration and for consenting women the slitting of the nose. The conference approved the new Order of the Temple (see page 73) and sent an appeal to Pope Calixtus II for a new crusade.

The response was limited but resources came from **Venice** – with the pope's agreement – and in 1124 the crusaders began to besiege the port of Tyre. Five months later, the town surrendered, leaving Ascalon as the only Muslim-held coastal port.

Venice

The city of Venice lies at the mouth of the river Po, its position at the head of the Adriatic Sea making a formidable situation. By the twelfth century it had developed into a powerful city state, trading between the West, the Byzantine Empire and the Muslim world. The head of the city was the **doge**, a member of the Great Council which governed the city, a position of power that was held for life. The power of the city state of Venice grew throughout the twelfth century and its wealth helped the crusader kingdom enormously, in return for increased trading privileges. The Venetian Empire grew to challenge the Byzantine Empire and eventually superseded it in the thirteenth century.

Source

(C)   **Trading privileges of the Venetians (1123–24), from William of Tyre's *Historia*. William of Tyre was chancellor of the kingdom of Jerusalem and probably copied this document direct from the royal archives when he wrote his *History* in the years 1170–85:**

For these privileges the Venetians need pay no tax whatever, whether according to custom or for any reason whatsoever, either on entering, staying, buying, selling either while remaining there or on departing. For no reason whatever need they pay any tax excepting only when they come or go, carrying pilgrims with their own vessels. Wherefore, the king of Jerusalem and all of us on behalf of the king agree to pay the doge of Venice, from the revenues of Tyre, on the feast day of the apostles of Peter and Paul, three hundred Saracen besants [gold coins] yearly, as agreed upon. Moreover, we promise you, doge of Venice, and your people that we will take nothing more from those nations who trade with you beyond what they are accustomed to give and as much as we receive from those who trade with other nations.

ACTIVITY
Period Studies

In terms of military leadership, how successful were Baldwin I and Baldwin II? Consider their territorial conquests, any battles and how they secured the new kingdom.

doge

In the republics of Venice and Genoa, the elected head of state.

ACTIVITY
Enquiries

Use Source C and your own knowledge to help you answer the following questions.

1   What taxes were the Venetians exempt from, according to Source C?

2   Why was the kingdom so generous in its exemptions and payments to Venice?

3   How useful is Source C as evidence for trading and commercial relations between the new kingdom and the West?

What were the crusader states?

The first 30 years for the outlying crusader states around the kingdom were years of continual campaigning. As well as being confronted by hostile Muslim forces, they were also troubled by internal disputes involving succession as the first generation of crusader leaders died.

Antioch was perhaps the most problematic of the crusader states, and the king of Jerusalem, Baldwin II, had to intervene frequently in its affairs in the years 1119–26. In theory, Edessa and Antioch were former states of the Byzantine Empire, but they were never handed over to the Emperor. The kingdom and the outlying states had not been part of any grand design by Pope Urban in 1095, or even by the crusaders in 1099 after they had captured Jerusalem.

It became apparent that the Christian communities needed protection, and the most famous leaders of the First Crusade – Baldwin, Godfrey, Bohemond and Raymond – remained in the Holy Land to govern them. All came from noble families, and they saw no reason not to create 'principalities' and 'counties' as they carved out the new territories over the years.

The Principality of Antioch

Antioch was in a more vulnerable position than Jerusalem, because of its proximity to the powerful Muslim lords of Aleppo and Homs in the east and the Seljuks to the north. Bohemond was captured by the Muslims in July 1100 and only released in 1103. In 1104 there was a battle at Harran and much land around Antioch was lost.

After the crusade of 1108, Bohemond returned to Italy, where he died in 1112, leaving a son, Bohemond II, who was too young to govern. Bohemond's cousin Tancred and then Roger of Salerno ruled on behalf of the young king, who eventually took power and married Alice, the daughter of King Baldwin II. In 1130, however, Bohemond II was himself killed. His head was sent to the Caliph of Baghdad.

The County of Edessa

This was the first crusader state, established by Baldwin of Boulogne. On becoming king of Jerusalem in 1100, Baldwin I passed the County of Edessa to his cousin, another Baldwin. This Baldwin was also to become king of Jerusalem in 1118 (Baldwin II), but before that he ruled Edessa and acted as regent for the young Bohemond II. After 1118 the county passed to a French family, the Courtenays, Joscelin I and Joscelin II. After the fall of Edessa in 1144, Joscelin II was captured by the Turks and died in an Aleppo dungeon.

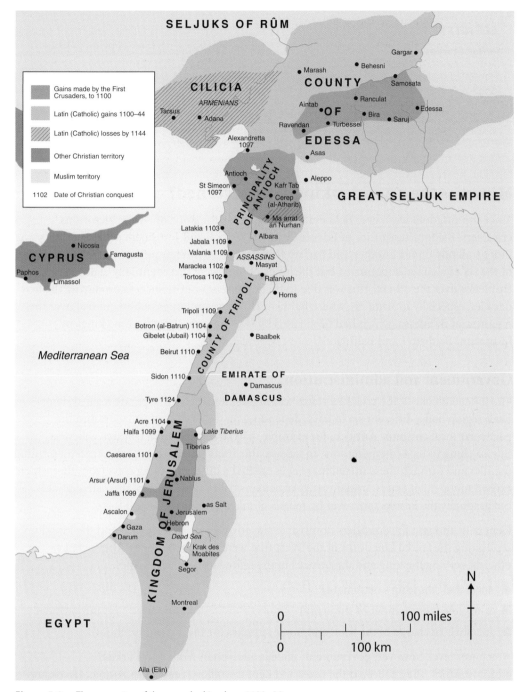

Figure 5.1 The expansion of the crusader kingdom, 1100–30.

The County of Tripoli

Raymond of Toulouse called himself Count of Tripoli, although he died in 1105 without ever having taken the town. The county began to form after the capture of Tortosa in 1101. After Raymond's death there was a succession dispute between Raymond's eldest son, Bertrand, and William Jordan, a cousin of Raymond. When William Jordan was killed soon afterwards, Bertrand and his son Pons took possession of the whole county.

5 How did the crusader kingdom develop and survive from 1100 to 1130?

ACTIVITY

Period Studies

To what extent did the internal weaknesses of the crusader states threaten the stability of the kingdom?

Before starting your answer, draw up a table with columns of evidence showing how the states' weaknesses threatened the kingdom's stability and how the problems were dealt with.

How was the crusader kingdom governed?

Since the kingdom was never deliberately designed by the Pope or by the victorious crusaders, the four territories of Edessa, Antioch, Tripoli and Jerusalem developed independently of one another and had no formal links to foreign powers in the West. None of the states claimed superiority, but the kings of Jerusalem did eventually claim pre-eminence over the others. This was due to the weaknesses of the succession during the first decades, especially in Antioch, where Baldwin II's intervention gave him control over the region, and in Edessa, which had been ruled by two men who later became kings of Jerusalem, Baldwin I and Baldwin II.

Government and administration

The independence of the crusader states was highlighted by their separate legal systems. Each region had a different set of laws, depending on the origins of its rulers and the particular local customs. Antioch, for example, had strong Norman features, whereas Edessa clung to its Armenian roots. In Edessa, the Franks married into the Armenian ruling families and through these mixed marriages created a different ruling class from that which existed in the other states. Initially, the Armenians held on to many of their strongholds, but gradually the Franks took over by means of marriage, purchase and force.

Generally, though, the crusaders dominated the governance of the states and the kingdom, replicating the feudal kingdoms of the West that were familiar to them. They acted as officials, serving the king and the princes in the following three capacities:

- seneschal (the king's lieutenant)
- constable (commander of the army)
- marshal (in charge of the food and horse supplies for the royal household).

At a lower level, however, government officials were often Arab and Turkish administrators. They collected the taxes and kept the official records in Arabic, Greek and Latin.

The feudal state

The king of Jerusalem was lord of Jerusalem, Tyre, Acre, Jaffa and Nablus. He could enfeoff lands to his vassals. He could also take them back, either in exchange for other lands or as a confiscation. However, a wise king would not upset his barons because he needed them and their knights in times of war. The overlordship of the king was exercised cautiously and with moderation. There were rebellions, but under Baldwin II the monarchy remained strong. The king had the right to choose husbands for the widows and unmarried daughters of his deceased vassals. Such marriages created cohesion within the nobility.

Family links with the West

The crusader kingdom's social links with the West were strong. Noble families in Europe sent their sons to Outremer deliberately to maintain the supply of nobles. The European nobility regarded the feudal kingdom of Outremer as a sort of province of feudal Europe, although no king or emperor in the West had formal powers over it. In theory, land was divided into fiefs, administered by the vassals who passed laws and defended the territory for their overlords. In practice, however, this varied from region to region, depending on the strength of the local customs. The territorial units of land around the crusaders' castles were garrisoned by troops who were bound by oaths of loyalty to their lords, just as in Europe. The flexibility and semi-independence of the crusader states were based on feudal customs of military service and loyalty. In times of crisis, the crusaders recognised common customs from their place of origin, and this contributed to the survival of the kingdom.

ACTIVITY

Period Studies

In what ways did the government of the new kingdom imitate the feudal systems and cultures of the West?

Include the following in your answer:

- the significance of the king
- the importance of the barons
- the government officials
- family ties with the West.

How significant was the lack of Muslim unity?

The fledgling kingdom of Outremer was always short of men and constantly under threat of attack from Muslim forces, but the Muslim armies remained disunited for the next 50 years. This was a major reason for the success of the First Crusade and the establishment of a Christian kingdom. The Fatimid Sunni Muslims of Egypt did not have common cause with the Shia of Aleppo and Damascus, who in turn had no solidarity with the Seljuk Turks of Asia Minor.

Although the crusader settlement was characterised by massacres and battles at places that included Jerusalem, Antioch and Tyre, outside the world of the military men, relations with the Muslim population had to be conducted by peaceful means, mainly because the Christians were so outnumbered that they could not risk betrayal and rebellion all the time. The population was incredibly diverse, and included western Europeans, Greeks, Armenians, Seljuks and Bedouin tribespeople. The Normans around Antioch had already conquered Muslim southern Sicily in 1091 and so were experienced in dealing with the process of colonisation. Trade and farming the land were vital to the survival and prosperity of the kingdom, and therefore it was in the interests of the westerners to allow the labourers and merchants to continue their work.

The Christian settlers therefore quickly assumed new identities, marrying local women and making their homes permanently in the East. The nobles of the new kingdom exploited the lack of Muslim unity by forming alliances with Muslims, sometimes against fellow Christians. When Tancred of Antioch and King Baldwin I clashed in 1105, both had

E

5 How did the crusader kingdom develop and survive from 1100 to 1130?

Turkish allies. In 1114, Roger of Antioch fought alongside Tughtigin of Damascus and Il Ghazi of Mardin to fight off Bursuq, commander of the Sultan's army from Baghdad. Such alliances contravened the ideals of holy war and the destruction of the 'infidel', but they were practical necessities at the time, even if the alliances did not last long.

Sources

D   Fulcher of Chartres, in his *History of the Expedition to Jerusalem*, written 1101–06, describes the situation in the Holy Land:

Baldwin possessed few cities and people. His enemies on all sides found out that he was a very skilful fighter. Although he had few men, his enemies did not dare attack him. Some Christian fighters remained in the Holy Land. Others went back to their native countries. For this reason the land of Jerusalem remained depopulated. There were not enough people to defend it from the Muslims if only the latter dared attack us. But they did not dare. It was a wonderful miracle that we lived among so many thousands and, as their conquerors, made some of them give us tribute and ruined others by plundering them and making them captives.

E   Al Sulami's *A Treatise*, written in 1105, comments on Christian successes:

The Christians looked down from their own lands on disunited Muslim kingdoms, whose hearts were in disagreement with differing opinions, linked with secret resentments. Thereby their ambitions grew in strength. They continued in the holy war against the Muslims, while the Muslims did not trouble about them or join forces to fight them. The Christians' hopes expanded as they saw their enemies content to be at peace with them.

ACTIVITY
Enquiries

Read Sources D and E and compare them as evidence for the significance of Muslim disunity. You will need to evaluate the origin and purpose of both sources and make a judgement on which one is more useful, but don't forget to consider the content.

The origins of the jihad

From the seventh to the eighth centuries the jihad (literally 'struggle', the Islamic holy war) developed in two forms. These were the internal spiritual struggle to achieve personal purity and the lesser, military struggle against the infidels – the Muslims saw it as their duty to get all the world to recognise or embrace Islam through conversion or subjugation. Both types of jihad were obligatory: jihad was fundamental to the Muslim faith, a spiritual as well as military exercise, a corporate not an individual obligation.

From the early eleventh century a blueprint had existed for ideology and action. The legal scholar al Sulami had urged moral reform within Islam as a preparation for the military reconquest, preaching at the great mosque in Damascus from his *Book of the Holy War*.

It was the resounding defeat of the crusaders at the Battle of the Field of Blood in 1119 which gave the Muslim world some hope that the Christians could be driven out. The first references to the jihad began to appear after 1119 on tombs and buildings. Tughtigin of Damascus was described in 1122 as 'protector of those who fight the holy war' and when he died in 1130 another memorial called him 'the prince, the one who fights the holy war, the one who perseveres assiduously on the frontier, the warrior.'

The crushing defeat of a crusader army and the killing of the prince of Antioch in 1119 gave the Arabs hope that they could destroy the Christians, but politically they were not ready to unite against their common foe.

ACTIVITY

Enquiries

Read Source F. How does the language used reflect its origin and affect its reliability?

Source

(F) **Kamal ad-Din was writing in the thirteenth century. He was based in Aleppo, and provided important material describing events in northern Syria. This extract is from his account of the Battle of the Field of Blood, in 1119:**

... the army swept down on the enemy tents, spreading chaos and destruction. God gave the victory to the Muslims. The Franks who fled to their camp were slaughtered. The Turks fought superbly, charging the enemy from every direction like one man. Arrows flew thick as locusts, and the Franks, with missiles raining down on infantry and cavalry alike, turned and fled ...

Even though the concept of the jihad was firmly established by c.1100, it was not transformed into concerted political and military action until after the capture of Jerusalem and the establishment of the crusader kingdom. In spite of the fact that some of the Muslim leaders were clearly identified as warriors of Islam, there was little concerted unity of effort to mount a well directed campaign against the new Christian kingdom. The lack of a great Muslim leader uniting the Muslims in battle under one banner was a major reason for the survival of the new kingdom in the first decades, as it had been for the capture of Jerusalem in 1099.

ACTIVITY

Period Studies

Why was it the Battle of the Field of Blood in 1119 and not the capture of Jerusalem in 1099 that changed the jihad from an intellectual to a military issue?

E

5 How did the crusader kingdom develop and survive from 1100 to 1130?

ACTIVITY

Enquiries

Use your own knowledge to assess how far Sources G to J support the view that the crusader kingdom developed mainly through co-operation between Christians and Muslims rather than by violence.

> Remember to think about the word 'mainly' in the question; is it one of several factors or is it the main reason?

Remember that this is a source paper and you should not simply write an essay about the relations between Christians and Muslims. Most of the marks available on this question will be awarded for using the sources and evaluating them to answer the question. If you want to achieve the higher levels, you must evaluate the sources and not simply use them to illustrate a point, so avoid writing 'Source J says'! You should also avoid simply going through each source and paraphrasing it.

On the positive side you must, having evaluated all the sources, reach a judgement – the examiner wants to know whether you think the crusader kingdom developed more through co-operation or violence. You must reach a decision and explain why.

Remember that you have already developed evaluation skills in comparing sources as evidence; you should not forget these skills when answering this question.

■ Have you considered the origin or author of the source and how it might affect the reliability?

■ Have you considered the purpose of the source and how it might affect the reliability?

■ Have you looked at the date of the source and how it might affect the reliability?

You also need to apply your own knowledge of the topic to evaluate the source. What do you know that either agrees or disagrees with what is said in the source? If you have knowledge that supports the interpretation in the sources, it is likely to make the source more reliable. On the other hand, if you have knowledge that disagrees with the interpretation in the source, it is likely to make the source less reliable. But remember that you may have knowledge that agrees with part of the source and disagrees with other parts.

To answer this question, you may find it helpful to draw up a table like the one below. Evaluate each source, deciding whether it agrees or disagrees with the idea that Christians and Muslims co-operated. Look carefully at the origin, purpose and language of each source, to help you make an assessment of all the sources. Make notes on how the kingdom and the states were established and compare them to the source evaluation you have made, to see whether or not the information supports the view that the crusader kingdom owed its existence more to co-operation than to violence. Come to a judgement on 'how far' before you begin writing your answer. It should help you to reach the higher levels as it will encourage you to group the sources and ascribe a relative value to each source. It is important to fill in both the 'for' and 'against' columns if the evidence justifies it, so that you see that sources can support different interpretations.

Source	Evaluation. How reliable is it?	For the assertion because:	Against the assertion because:
G			
H			
I			
J			

Sources

G An anonymous Muslim poet from the early twelfth century responds to the crusade and the new Christian kingdom:

The sword is cutting and the blood is spilt.

How many Muslim men have become booty?

And how many Muslim women's inviolability has been plundered?

How many a mosque have they made into a church!

The cross has been set up in the mihrab [niche in the wall of the mosque facing Mecca]

The blood of a pig is suitable for it.*

Qurans have been burned under the guise of incense.

Do you not owe an obligation to God and Islam,

Defending thereby young men and old?

Respond to God: woe on you! Respond!

*Pigs are seen as unclean and it is forbidden in Muslim and Jewish religious law to eat pigs. The 'blood of a pig' is therefore a grave insult.

H Fulcher of Chartres' *History of Jerusalem* (written 1095–1127):

He who was a Roman [Italian] or a Frank [Frenchman] has, in this land, been made into a Galilean or a Palestinian. He who was of Rheims or Chartres has now become a citizen of Tyre or Antioch. We have already forgotten the places of our birth … some already possess homes or household by inheritance. Some have taken wives not only of their own people, but Syrians, Armenian, or even Saracens who have achieved the grace of baptism. He who was born a stranger is now as one born here; he who was born an alien has become a native. Our relatives and parents join us from time to time, sacrificing, even reluctantly, all that they formerly possessed.

I Usama Ibn Munqidh (1095–1188), was a Muslim warrior and a resident of the area around Palestine, who befriended a number of the crusaders:

There was in Antioch at that time al Ra'is Theodoros Sophianos, to whom I was bound by mutual ties of amity. His influence in Antioch was supreme. One day he said to my man, 'I am invited by a friend of mine who is a Frank. Thou shouldst come with me so that thou may see their fashions.' My man related the story in the following words:

'I went along with him and we came to the home of a knight who belonged to the old category of knights who came with the early expeditions of the Franks. He had been by that time stricken off the register and exempted from service, and possessed in Antioch an estate on the income of which he lived. The knight presented an excellent table, with food extraordinarily clean and delicious. Seeing me abstaining from food, he said, "Eat, be of good cheer! I never eat Frankish dishes, but I have Egyptian women cooks and never eat except their cooking. Besides, pork never enters my home." I ate, but guardedly, and after that we departed.'

J Jean Richard, *The Crusades c.1071–c.1291*:

In the case of the Muslims we need to distinguish between the time of conquest and their later situation within the Frankish states. During the conquest, they suffered badly. The capture of fortified towns entailed violence and massacres, some of which have been described in lavish detail, for Jerusalem, Ma'arrat, Caiphas or Beirut among others. When a town was stormed, such excesses were sadly only too common. Of the women captured in Caesarea, conquered in 1104, the historian tells us that 'beautiful or ugly, they had to turn the grindstone of the mills' that is, they became domestic slaves.

Richard, J. (1999). *The Crusades, c.1071–c.1291.* Cambridge: Cambridge University Press.

Conclusion

By 1130 the new kingdom and the provinces were well established. The familiar concept of a king had been replicated in the new kingdom and a dynasty put in place. New conquests had secured the coastline and the three provinces of Tripoli, Antioch and Edessa were created. The governance of the kingdom in theory imitated western traditions of kingship and feudal hierarchies, but in reality drew upon a range of local customs and laws. However, the survival of the new kingdom and its outlying states was by no means assured

5 How did the crusader kingdom develop and survive from 1100 to 1130?

and several measures had to be put in place to ensure its survival, and we will look at these in the next chapter.

Review questions

Plan your answers by creating two columns headed 'for' and 'against' in note form. Make a judgement before you begin writing and distinguish clearly between the two sides of the argument. In questions 1, 2 and 4 you will need to make a judgement on 'how far' or to what extent, weighing up two sides of the argument but remembering to include the lesser aspect of the answer. In question 3, you are making an assessment of a factor, so you will need to look at that factor in the wider context of power and government in order to assess how important the king actually was, before making your judgement.

1 How far was the lack of Muslim unity the main reason for the survival of the kingdom?

2 To what extent was the kingdom a coherent political unit?

3 Assess the importance of the role of the king of Jerusalem.

4 To what extent were the Christian and Muslim communities successfully integrated?

How did the crusader kingdom develop into a military state between 1100 and 1130?

Key Questions:

In this chapter you will learn:

- Why castles were important
- How the new military orders helped to defend the kingdom

You will also develop the following skills:

- Assessing the language and tone of documents with reference to the 'new knighthood' of the Military Orders
- Comparing sources and their limitations
- Understanding the major conceptual shift from the 'armed pilgrims' of 1095 to the fighting monks of the new Orders by 1130

Introduction

It has been shown that the kingdom of Jerusalem and its outlying states of Tripoli, Antioch and Edessa developed rapidly and with varying degrees of success in the period 1100–30. The chief reason for the survival of the crusader kingdom was the lack of Muslim unity. However, after the Battle of the Field of Blood in 1119, both sides realised that stronger military actions could result in outright defeat of the enemy. The crusader kingdom therefore needed to develop into a military as well as a political state.

It did this in the following ways:

- The crusaders built castles in the form of massive stone fortresses in the desert, forming a defensive ring around the soft underbelly of the Holy City, which had little strategic or economic value.
- The chronic problem of manpower was solved to an extent by the foundation of the military orders of the Knights Templars and the Knights Hospitallers.

KEY ISSUES

- Why were castles built?
- How significant were the military orders?

Chapter timeline

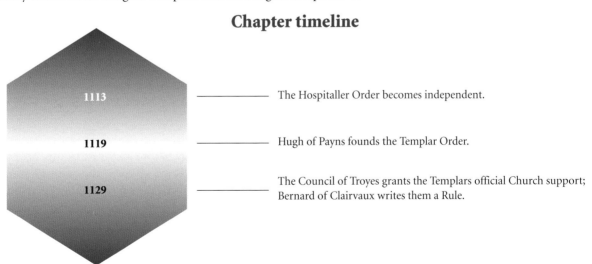

1113	The Hospitaller Order becomes independent.
1119	Hugh of Payns founds the Templar Order.
1129	The Council of Troyes grants the Templars official Church support; Bernard of Clairvaux writes them a Rule.

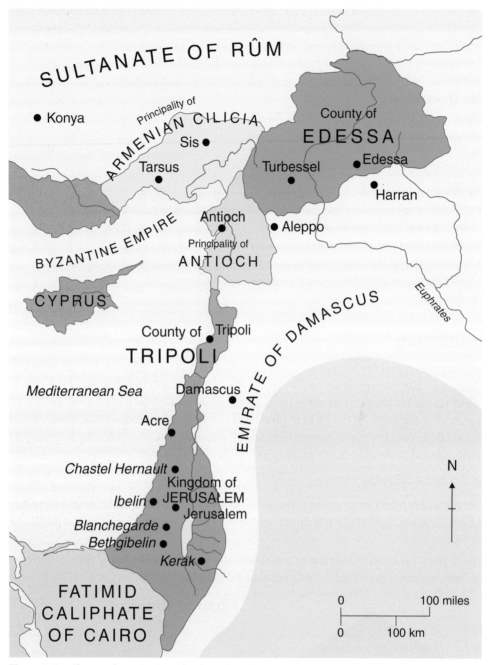

Figure 6.1: The crusader territories and early castles, 1100–30.

Why were castles built?

No king could afford to lose the support of his feudal barons and their troops, because the crusader kingdom was in a state of perpetual struggle for survival. The occupation of Outremer was based on the fortifications which ensured the survival of the kingdom. Castles primarily had a military function, such as to defend a mountain pass, to dominate a valley, or to intimidate and gradually strangle a Muslim town or fortification. They also had administrative and commercial functions, acting as centres of local government and protecting trade routes and markets.

The crusaders found many Byzantine and Arab fortifications which they restored and enlarged, but they also built many new and impressive castles during the twelfth century. From the very beginning, to keep the Egyptian garrison at Ascalon penned in, the castles of Chastel Hernault, Ibelin, Blanchegarde and Bethgibelin were constructed. King Baldwin I built Montreal to control the valleys across to the Dead Sea and the Gulf of Aqaba. Kerak was the great castle which controlled the land of the Oultrejourdain in the far south, supervising the pilgrim and trade routes between Damascus and Egypt. To the north, castles were built to defend the passes of the Lebanon, and the Krak des Chevaliers, the greatest of all crusader castles, commanded the Homs valley and the approaches to the coastal plains from southern Syria.

Each castle was at the centre of a region which supplied it with food and rents so that the commanders could pay their garrisons. Most commanders lived inside the castle walls. By contrast, Muslim fortifications were urban, with impressive walls, gateways and citadels such as those at Damascus and Aleppo.

Figure 6.2   Krak des Chevaliers, the greatest of all the crusader castles, was built in the mid-twelfth century.

The chain of crusader castles defending the valleys ('wadis') and coastal plains was impressive, but the shortage of men meant that the leaders were faced with the choice of deploying them either to defend a castle or to go onto the battlefield, which was a high-risk strategy. The private and remote nature of the crusader castles – in contrast with the Muslim fortified towns – meant that the Christian forces could be bottled up and surrounded in times of major invasion. For the time being, however, in the period when Muslim forces were not united against the crusaders, the castles dominated the landscape and consolidated the conquest of the Holy Land.

P/E

6 How did the crusader kingdom develop into a military state between 1100 and 1130?

ACTIVITY

Period Studies

How important were crusader castles in the early years of the kingdom?

Source

(A) **William of Tyre, writing in the 1180s, describes how castle garrisons avoided battle:**

The knights of the Temple who lived in the same vicinity also remained shut up in their strongholds; they expected almost hourly to be besieged and did not wish to risk an encounter with the Turks. The brothers of the Hospital had likewise retired in alarm to their fortified castle of Krak. During this time Saladin ranged here and there over the plain, especially the cultivated fields, and without opposition traversed the entire locality. He burned all the crops, those that had been gathered into the granaries, those still stacked in the field, and the growing grain as well. He drove off cattle as booty and laid waste the whole country in every direction.

ACTIVITY

Enquiries

Read Source A and answer the following questions.

1   Why did the Templars not want to risk an encounter with the Turks?

2   How useful for us is William of Tyre's description of the strengths and weaknesses of castles and the crusaders?

Battle-avoidance

The traditional view of the Middle Ages was that society was constantly at war and that armies were forever slaughtering one another in battle. However, we now understand that medieval battles were actually quite rare. Put simply, it was too risky for kings, dukes and nobles to fight battles; defeat meant the slaughter of the soldiers and possible death or capture (and disgrace) of the leaders. Military might was demonstrated instead by castles, lightning raids and ambushes. Negotiations and truces were far more common than battle, which was the last resort.

How significant were the military orders?

The crusader kingdom of Outremer was surviving and developing, but there was a constant shortage of men to garrison the newly built castles and to guard the pilgrim and trade routes. During the period 1100–30, two new institutions emerged which were to change the face of holy war and alter the political landscape of the kingdom. These were the orders of warrior-monks, the Knights Templars and the Knights Hospitallers, whose function was to protect pilgrims and provide military manpower to defend the crusader kingdom. The concept of a fighting monk was another radical shift from Pope Urban's preaching of 1095, which had sanctioned the killing of fellow men, albeit non-Christians. The warrior-monks were members of religious orders, sworn to chastity, poverty and obedience, but instead of spending their time in prayer, contemplation and copying out manuscripts, they manned castles, raided Muslim territory and took lives, often losing their own in the process.

The Templars

The Templars were so called because King Baldwin II had provided them with accommodation in the remains of the Jewish temple in Jerusalem. The order was founded in 1119 by Hugh of Payns, a French nobleman, but initially they had been a group of laymen, not monks. Its foundation was probably prompted by the disastrous defeat of the crusaders at the Battle of the Field of Blood in June 1119 (see page 58) and the slaughter of 300 pilgrims near the River Jordan at Easter in the same year. The idea of a body of men dedicated to defending pilgrims attracted the attention of Count Fulk of Anjou, who stayed with them for a year in 1120 (he later became king of Jerusalem in 1131). Hugh of Payns travelled to Europe to gain wider support and the notion of fighting monks emerged, whereby the Templars would supply a permanent troop of committed warriors in the Holy Land. **Bernard of Clairvaux** wrote a Rule (a way of life) for the order and requested papal approval for them. In January 1129 the Church gave its support at the Council of Troyes and soon afterwards money, land and men all flocked to the order. The King of Aragon, Alfonso I, even donated his entire kingdom (this was not practical, but large grants nevertheless were made).

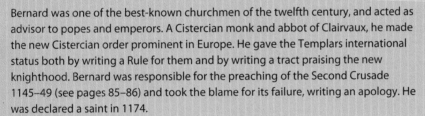

BIOGRAPHY
Bernard of Clairvaux (1090–1153)

Bernard was one of the best-known churchmen of the twelfth century, and acted as advisor to popes and emperors. A Cistercian monk and abbot of Clairvaux, he made the new Cistercian order prominent in Europe. He gave the Templars international status both by writing a Rule for them and by writing a tract praising the new knighthood. Bernard was responsible for the preaching of the Second Crusade 1145–49 (see pages 85–86) and took the blame for its failure, writing an apology. He was declared a saint in 1174.

What was the Rule of the Templars?

Bernard of Clairvaux deliberately based the Templars' Rule on the Augustinian, rather than the Benedictine Rule. This meant that it was more worldly-wise, and included detail on the behaviour of knights in battle, discipline, equipment and the hierarchy of the order, as well as the fundamental monastic concepts of chastity, poverty and obedience. The Templars were to live a communal life of discipline and obedience, focusing on their duties to God to assist their commitment in battle.

How radical was the Templar Order?

The concept of warrior-monks was a clear step forward from the 'just war' theories of 1095 where Christian knights were urged to kill unbelievers. Bernard called the Templars the 'soldiers of Christ', a new sort of knight whose purpose was to defend the Holy Land and destroy evil. Bernard was so conscious of the novelty of the warrior-monks that he wrote a document defending the notion of a monk killing people, contrasting the new soldiers of Christ with the lustful, vainglorious and senseless killers of old, whose search for booty and plunder was a discredit to the new knighthood.

E

6 How did the crusader kingdom develop into a military state between 1100 and 1130?

ACTIVITY

Enquiries

Read Sources B and C.

1   Explain the following phrases in Source B:

- 'salvation of your souls'
- 'scorn the temptations of your body'
- 'the food of God'.

2   What language does Bernard of Clairvaux use in both sources to stress the Templars' military purpose, even though they are monks?

Sources

B From the *Rule of the Templars*, Bernard of Clairvaux, 1129:

You who renounce your own wills, and you others serving the sovereign king with horses and arms, for the salvation of your souls strive everywhere with pure desire to hear matins and the entire service according to canonical law and the customs of the regular masters of the Holy City of Jerusalem. O you venerable brothers, similarly God is with you, if you promise to despise the deceitful world in perpetual love of God, and scorn the temptations of your body: sustained by the food of God and watered and instructed in the commandments of Our Lord, at the end of the divine office, none should fear to go into battle if he henceforth wears the **tonsure**.

C From *In praise of the New Knighthood*, Bernard of Clairvaux, c.1130:

First, they are disciplined and obedient ... They live as brothers in joyful and sober company, without wives or children. So that their spiritual perfections will lack nothing, they dwell in one family without any personal property ... They never sit idly nor wander aimlessly ... They forswear dice and chess. I do not know if it is more appropriate to call them monks or knights, perhaps it is better to recognise them as being both, for they lack neither monastic meekness nor military fortitude. God chose these men whom he recruited from the ends of the earth; they are valiant men of Israel chosen to guard the tomb of Solomon, each man, sword in hand, superbly trained to conduct war.

tonsure

Monks all had a distinctive haircut which shaved the middle of the head, leaving a fringe all around.

indulgence

In the medieval Catholic Church, a reduction of or exemption from punishment for sins committed during one's life.

How did the power of the Templars develop during the twelfth century?

In the years 1139–45 the Templars gained privileges from the papacy which secured them the right to elect their own master, exemption from the taxes payable to the local church and the right to appoint their own priests. There were inducements for the lay nobility, too: anyone granting land, money or goods to the Templars would receive a papal **indulgence**, and if a layman became a Templar towards the end of his life (or even on his deathbed) then he could be buried in the Templar cemetery.

As the power of the Templars grew, they were given lands and castles in Outremer, from the late 1130s, near Antioch in the north and Gaza in the south. Local churchmen did not always accept the Templars' power, but the support from the pope in Rome made the Templars virtually untouchable. The Templars also clashed with the secular rulers, but here also, their immunity from secular jurisdiction meant that any misdemeanours they committed had to be tried in Rome.

> ### Source
>
> (D) **William of Tyre, writing 1170–74, describes the wealth of the Templars:**
>
> *They have now grown so great that there are in this Order today about 300 knights who wear white mantles, in addition to the brothers [i.e. those non-combatant monks], who are almost countless. They are said to have immense possessions both here and overseas, so that there is now not a province in the Christian world which has not bestowed upon the aforesaid brothers a portion of its goods. It is said today that their wealth is equal to the treasures of kings.*

ACTIVITY

Enquiries

Read Sources C and D. In what ways did the Templars change? Consider their numbers, their role and purpose and their growing influence.

The idea of fighting monks was not universally accepted. Their special privileges and exemption from taxes were seen as an encouragement to acquire wealth and power that were unsuited to spiritual men. John of Salisbury, one of the great intellectuals of the twelfth century, felt that the knightly and clerical functions of the Templars were incompatible. Indeed, the actions of the Templars were to cause many problems for the kings of Jerusalem and crusade leaders in the future. In 1153, for example, a group of Templars broke into the Muslim-held town of Ascalon ahead of the main Christian army and apparently refused to let the rest of the army inside because they wanted the booty for themselves. (They were then trapped in the town, surrounded and massacred by the Muslims.) The power of the Templar Order was unchecked, however, and was a major factor in the crisis of 1187 (see pages 111–12).

The Hospitallers

The Order of the Hospital of St John of Jerusalem, the Knights Hospitallers, was the other order of fighting monks. Its origin was earlier and rather different from that of the Templars. It began in the mid-eleventh century, therefore pre-dating the crusades, as a **hospice** run by Italian traders caring for sick pilgrims in a building alongside the church of the Holy Sepulchre in Jerusalem. After the crusaders captured Jerusalem in 1099, Godfrey of Bouillon became an early supporter of the Hospitallers, and the flood of pilgrims now entering Jerusalem added to their importance. Daughter hospices were founded in southern France, Sicily, Spain, Italy and England in the years 1100–30, with landed estates organised around a village, a church, a hospital and a farm, called commanderies, which sent funds to the East to support the hospices there. These commanderies were grouped into priories. The General Chapter, the leading men of the order, met in the Holy Land. The scale of the order's endowments, donations and manpower grew rapidly, and was a vital supply line to the warrior-monks and hospitals in the East. It is estimated that in 1169 there were 1000 beds in the main Hospital in Jerusalem, maintained at an enormous cost.

In 1113, the Hospitallers became an independent order. Pope Paschal II issued a **papal bull** which gave them papal protection and allowed them freedom to elect their own master. The Rule of the Hospital was written in the years 1120–60 and was based on Augustinian principles, like the Rule of the Templars. It regulated a communal life and provided instructions for its members on vows, discipline, administrative matters and care of the sick and poor. Like the Templars, the Hospitallers took vows of poverty, chastity and obedience, but in the early stages, there were no knights.

hospice

In medieval times, a lodging for travellers and pilgrims, run by a religious order.

papal bull

An official order from the pope.

P/E

6 How did the crusader kingdom develop into a military state between 1100 and 1130?

ACTIVITY

Enquiries

Using Source E and your own knowledge, say what the differences were between the Templars and the Hospitallers.

Source

(E) **An anonymous account of the treatment of the sick in the Hospital of St John, Jerusalem, written in the 1120s:**

It was ordained by the master of the Hospital and by the General Chapter that each patient should have each day half a soft loaf and sufficient house bread, and the same wine as the convent. The doctors should observe closely the qualities of the sick and what illnesses they have, and should inspect their urine and give syrups and other things which may be necessary for sick people ... among the wards are to be brothers who keep watch at night, that is to say two brothers who are to keep watch each night in order that nothing adverse should happen to our sick lords.

ACTIVITY

Period Studies

To what extent were the military orders different from the 'armed pilgrims' of the First Crusade?

The emergence of the military Hospitallers

Probably encouraged by the rise of the Templar Order, which was military in function from the beginning, the Hospitallers gradually assumed a knightly role. In 1136 King Fulk granted them the castle of Bethgibelin and by 1144 they had control of the fortress at Krak des Chevaliers. The Hospitallers' military role increased rapidly in the 1160s, so much so that they were determining policy against the Muslims. Like the Templars, they were to court controversy and play a major part the political faction and divisions in the kingdom in the 1180s.

ACTIVITY

Enquiries

1 Compare Sources F and G as evidence for the lack of military manpower in the crusader kingdom. You will need to evaluate the origin and purpose of both sources and make a judgement on which one is more useful. You will also need to compare the content of the two sources, point by point.

2 Use your own knowledge to assess how far Sources F to J support the view that castles were the most significant reason for developing crusader military power in the period 1100–30.

Remember to think about the words 'most significant'; is it one of several factors or is it the most significant reason?

To answer question 2, you may find it helpful to draw up a table like the one below. First, put each source into a column, either agreeing or disagreeing that castles were the most significant reason, looking carefully at origin, purpose and language to help you assess the source. Make notes on the nature of warfare and the military orders and compare them to the source evaluation you have made, to see whether or not the information supports the view of castles as the most significant reason. Come to a judgement on 'how far' before you begin writing your answer.

Source	Evaluation. How reliable is it?	For the assertion because:	Against the assertion because:
F			
G			
H			
I			
J			

Source

F **Walter the Chancellor, writing 1114–22, was an eyewitness from the Principality of Antioch. He describes the Muslim tactic of drawing the crusader forces out into a single battle to defeat them. The crusaders were constantly short of men and had to wait for reinforcements before committing to battle, if they did so at all:**

Therefore the Persians [i.e. the Muslims] marvelled that a race so ready for war and always intolerant of injury, who had been provoked so often by arrows, afflicted so often by jeers, was so long-suffering, because the Christians did not signal the start of battle and were already submitting as if fear had conquered them. Some of our men even considered it an act of cowardice; however some of greater perspicacity interpreted it as the purpose of the prince [Roger of Antioch] so that, when he was sure the time was right, they would be stronger to attack, not at the enemy's summoning, nor in anticipation of their forces, but by the prudent disposition and enormous experience of himself and the king …

G **In his *History of the Expedition to Jerusalem*, Fulcher of Chartres, writing in 1127, describes a stand-off between the Christian and Muslim armies in 1118:**

There assembled a very large army of horsemen and infantry with the intention of destroying the Christians of Jerusalem in battle. Tughtigin, the King of Damascus, advanced to aid them with his men. Then King Baldwin of Jerusalem with the men of Antioch hurried off to do battle against the hostile army. But because each side greatly feared to attack the other, for nearly three months both sides managed to postpone fighting for reasons of this kind. Then the Muslims, worn out by the delay, abandoned the war.

H **William of Tyre, writing in the 1180s, describes the gradual encirclement of Muslim-held Ascalon in the 1140s by crusader castles:**

Our people resolved to erect fortifications around about [Ascalon]. Within these strongholds forces could easily be assembled which, from their very proximity would check the enemy's forays. Such fortresses would serve as bases to make frequent attacks upon the city itself. Often by themselves, more often in company with men at arms from the other fortresses built with similar intent, these men issued forth to encounter and defeat the enemy when they tried to make raids from the city. The whole district became much more secure because the locality was occupied and a more abundant supply of food for the surrounding country was made possible.

I **From *In praise of the New Knighthood*, by Bernard of Clairvaux, written around 1130:**

When the battle is at hand, they arm themselves inwardly with faith and outwardly with steel rather than with decorations of gold, since their business is to strike fear in the enemy rather than to incite cupidity [envy]. No matter how outnumbered they are never awed by the fierce enemy hordes. Nor do they overestimate their own strength, but trust in the Lord to grant them victory.

J **From Jonathan Phillips, *The Crusades, 1095–1197*:**

While battles could exert a decisive influence on Frankish power, the key to holding on to territory was the control of castles and fortified sites, which included towns and rural manor houses. The knowledge gained in the course of the [first] crusade proved invaluable in taking the other castles and fortifications of the Levant, as the Franks established their rule. It was then the settlers who had to refortify, develop and construct their own defences in order to preserve their hold on the Holy Land and to provide centres of authority.

Phillips, J. (2002). *The Crusades, 1095–1197.* Harlow: Longman.

Figure 6.3   The seal of the Knights Templars. The two men on one horse represented the Templars' vow of poverty, though the poverty of the order did not last very long.

Conclusion: how secure was the crusader kingdom in 1130?

The emergence of the military orders marked another radical shift in western thinking. Here were men who were dedicated to the destruction of Islam. They were feared by the Muslims, who executed them whenever they were captured, whereas other captured crusader knights and soldiers might be imprisoned, sold into slavery or ransomed. The military orders provided vital troops to Outremer and in time accrued vast reserves of wealth and power, way beyond their original aims as poor knights and medical aids. The establishment of the military orders reflects how far the situation in the Holy Land had shifted from Pope Urban II's vision in 1095, to become a permanent institution with laws, borders and internal politics.

Since the capture of Jerusalem, the new kingdom had developed over 30 years without a plan or design into an established region with provinces, nobles, fortifications and a system of government and administration. Many of those who settled in the kingdom of Outremer quickly assimilated with the local customs and landscape. The strength of Baldwin I and Baldwin II laid firm foundations, supported by the efforts of Bohemond, Tancred and Roger of Antioch. The chronic shortage of manpower would be eased to some extent by the new military orders of the Templars and Hospitallers. The defeat at the Battle of the Field of Blood in 1119 had revealed the vulnerability of the kingdom. The outlying states were constantly engaged in a struggle for survival, but the building of castles made a major impact on the survival of the kingdom. The weaknesses of the kingdom would be exploited by its enemies after 1130, culminating in the efforts of Nur ad-Din (1145–74) and Saladin (1174–93), but the military developments of the first three decades had ensured its success.

Review questions

1   Assess the view that castles were the primary military weapon of the Holy Land. In answering this question, you should look at all the military tactics used in The Holy Land, including battles, sieges and raids, as well as castles, so that you can place castles in a wider context in order to make your judgement.

2   How far did the creation of the military orders help to solve the problems of the crusader kingdom? You will need to make a judgement here on 'how far', and to do this you need to look at both points of view – positive and negative – regarding the help the Orders provided, before you can make a judgement.

What was the impact of the Second Crusade?

7

Key Questions:

In this chapter you will learn:

- How the weaknesses in the crusader kingdom helped the Muslims to conquer Edessa
- Why the Second Crusade failed

You will also develop the following skills:

- Assessing the language and tone of documents
- Comparing sources and their limitations
- Understanding the short-term weaknesses and divisions of the kingdom
- Making a judgement on why the Second Crusade failed

Introduction

On 24 December 1144, the Muslim ruler of Aleppo and Mosul, Imad ad-Din Zengi, captured the outlying crusader state of Edessa, the first state to be established in 1098. The crusader kingdom had suffered internal divisions over the succession of King Fulk (1131–43) and

Chapter timeline

1134	Count Hugh of Jaffa's rebellion.
1144	Zengi captures the crusader state of Edessa.
1145	Pope Eugenius III launches the Second Crusade.
1146	The armies of King Louis VII of France and Emperor Conrad of Germany depart.
1146	Second attack on Edessa, destroying much of the city.
1147	German army wiped out in Asia Minor.
1148	Louis VII attacks Damascus and fails to capture it; end of the crusade.

there had been external threats from the Byzantine Empire over the control of Antioch. Zengi's conquest of Edessa was a severe blow. It prompted the sending of letters to the West. appealing for help. These appeals for help provoked the Second Crusade, a major expedition led by the king of France, Louis VII, and the German emperor, Conrad. The pope, Eugenius III, saw this as an opportunity to regain command of the crusading movement and to inspire a new generation of armed pilgrims. However, clashes between the settler-crusaders and the westerners, the Greeks and the military orders, and the lack of an objective as clear and appealing as Jerusalem, resulted in failure to recapture Edessa. This in turn served to encourage greater Muslim unity, to lower morale amongst the settler-crusaders and damage the standing of the papacy.

> **KEY ISSUES**
>
> ■ How far was the kingdom weakened by internal divisions 1130–44?
>
> ■ Why was Zengi able to take Edessa?
>
> ■ What was the response of the West?
>
> ■ In what ways was the Second Crusade different from the First?
>
> ■ Why did the Second Crusade fail?
>
> ■ Who was to blame for the failure of the Second Crusade?

How far was the kingdom weakened by internal divisions 1130–44?

Baldwin II's successful reign (1119–31) was marred by concerns about who would succeed him: he had four daughters and no surviving son. The king and his nobles agreed that Count Fulk V of Anjou, in France, would marry the eldest daughter, **Melisende**, and become king of Jerusalem on Baldwin's death. Fulk, who had already spent a year with the Templars in 1120–21, accepted in 1128 and the couple had a son, Baldwin, in 1130. The succession was assured and Fulk took power in 1131 without any problems.

> **BIOGRAPHY**
> **Queen Melisende of Jerusalem (1131–52)**
>
> Eldest daughter of King Baldwin II and his Armenian wife, married to Count Fulk of Anjou. Melisende was an astute politician, who limited Fulk's efforts to promote his Angevin favourites. After Fulk's death, she continued to rule until her son, Baldwin III (then only thirteen) came of age.

How dangerous was the rebellion of Count Hugh?

In 1134 a rebellion led by Count Hugh of Jaffa revealed that all was not well with the native crusader nobles and the outsider King Fulk. Rumour had it that Hugh was too friendly with Queen Melisende, and when Hugh was accused of treason he fled the court. He refused a trial by combat, and made a deal with the Muslims of Ascalon, provoking the king to march south and besiege Jaffa. Hugh was forced into exile but was stabbed while waiting to leave the Holy Land – he died in Apulia (Italy). Whatever the truth behind the accusations,

Hugh's fatal stabbing gained him much sympathy and forced Fulk to consult more closely with the Queen and the native crusaders. The story of the romance between Hugh and Melisende may not be true, but Fulk's over-promotion of outsiders (his own people from France) did antagonise the native crusaders, and it had been Hugh who led the revolt. Fulk favoured his people from France because Baldwin II had insisted that the kingdom should be ruled by Queen Melisende, Fulk and their son, Baldwin, when he grew up, which Fulk obviously found too limiting.

Sources

A William of Tyre (writing 1170–85, in the Holy Land), gives an insider's view:

For certain reasons, some of the highest nobles of the realm, namely, Hugh, Count of Jaffa, are said to have conspired against the lord king … Some said that the king cherished a deep mistrust of the count who was rumoured to be on too familiar terms with the queen, and of this there seemed to be many proofs … One day, Walter of Caesarea … at the instigation of the king himself, it was claimed, publicly accused Hugh of high treason … Single combat was decreed according to the custom of the Franks and a suitable day was set for the combat. The count then left the court and returned to Jaffa. The assembly of nobles condemned him in his absence as guilty of the charge against him.

B Orderic Vitalis, writing in Normandy in the 1130s, got his evidence from returning pilgrims:

To begin with he [Fulk] acted without the foresight and shrewdness he should have shown, and changed governors and other dignitaries too quickly and thoughtlessly. As a new ruler he banished from his counsels the leading magnates who from the first had fought resolutely against the Turks and helped Godfrey and the two Baldwins to bring towns and fortresses under their rule, and replaced them with Angevin strangers and other raw newcomers to whom he gave his ear … Consequently great disaffection spread … they even allied on both sides with the pagans against each other, with the result that they lost many thousands of men and a certain number of fortresses.

ACTIVITY

Compare Sources A and B as evidence for the rebellion of 1134.

Were relations with the Byzantine Empire a problem?

In Antioch there was another succession dispute caused by the death of Prince Bohemond II, who left a daughter, Constance. Bohemond's widow, Alice, ruled in her own right, but stability only came to Antioch when Constance married Raymond of Poitiers in 1136. However, in 1137–38 and 1142–43 the Byzantine emperor, John Comnenus, appeared with an army, claiming his ancient rights as overlord of Antioch that had existed over the territory before the First Crusade. Raymond swore homage to him and acknowledged that his lands were under Byzantine lordship. There was no Byzantine attack on Antioch, as Emperor John was wary of bringing a western crusade down on his head. However, the events reflected the lack of unity between the Byzantine Empire and the crusaders, and was a reminder of the uneasy relations between them.

Why was Zengi able to take Edessa?

It was precisely during this time of uncertainty in the 1130s and 1140s that the atabeg of Mosul and Aleppo, Zengi, developed his power ruthlessly and dominantly in the region, raiding Christian and Muslim lands. In December 1144 he laid siege to the city of Edessa and on 24 December he took the city and went on to gain much territory east of the River Euphrates.

Zengi's main ambition was not in fact Edessa but Damascus. The emir of Damascus formed a treaty with the crusaders in 1140, which illustrates the nature of alliances of Christian and Muslim against Muslim (see page 48). This treaty between Jerusalem and Damascus forced

Zengi to look north, and when King Fulk of Jerusalem died in a hunting accident in 1143, Queen Melisende and her young son Baldwin were in no position to defend the north. When Zengi laid siege to Edessa in late 1144, the city was only defended by Archbishop Hugh, who was short of money. Zengi moved fast, before other crusaders could come to the aid of Edessa's inhabitants. His troops built wooden towers, dug tunnels under the town walls and bombarded the walls until they collapsed. Eventually the town was taken: 15,000 people were slaughtered, including Archbishop Hugh; the town was sacked, the churches and monasteries were destroyed.

Edessa had fallen mainly due to its remote situation and the speed of Zengi's attack, but the lack of support from the Byzantine forces and the divided crusader factions was significant.

> ## Source
>
> **William of Tyre, writing in the 1170s, describes the fall of Edessa:**
>
> *Zengi, meanwhile, pressed continual assaults on the city. He ran the gamut of attacks and left nothing untried which could harass the citizens and aid him in gaining control of the city. He sent sappers through trenches and underground tunnels to undermine the walls. As they dug passages beneath the walls, they buttressed these with posts, which were afterward set on fire. A great part of the wall was thus broken down. This breach in the wall, more than 100 cubits wide, gave the enemy an entrance into the city. Their forces rushed together into the city. They slew with their swords the citizens whom they encountered, sparing neither age, condition, nor sex. The city, therefore, was captured and delivered to the swords of the enemy.*

ACTIVITY

How accurate is Source C in explaining the capture of Edessa? Use the source and your own knowledge to make this judgement.

What were the achievements of Zengi?

Zengi was a Turk who sought to dominate the Arab emirs and princes in Syria. As with the crusaders, so with the Muslim tribal leaders: religion gave authority to political ambitions, and Zengi was portrayed as a champion of the jihad by his supporters. The jihad revival relied on Islamic intellectual and spiritual movements being translated into political ambition and action. Zengi the warlord was surrounded by poets and scholars urging their fellow Muslims to embark on the jihad against the crusaders, and he became the focus of holy war ideology and recruitment.

Jihad rhetoric was partly a religious revival and partly good politics. Religious leaders encouraged holy war as an Islamic duty, and at the same time it suited political leaders to expand their territory. Zengi was most concerned with crushing his Muslim enemies; he used the jihad as a means of constructing alliances. He was not a pious Muslim and his murder perhaps reflected the violence that characterised his actions.

Zengi was assassinated in September 1146, leaving Edessa to the crusaders. However, his son, Nur ad-Din, Prince of Aleppo, launched a new attack on the town of Edessa before the crusaders could repair the damage Zengi had done to its fortifications. Tens of thousands were slaughtered or enslaved.

> ## Source
>
> **D** **Ibn al-Athir, writing in the 1230s, praises Zengi:**
>
> *Before he came to power the absence of strong rulers to impose justice, and the presence of the Franks close at hand, had made the country a wilderness, but he made it flower again. The population increased and so did its prosperity. Mosul had been one of the most impoverished regions before Zengi's time, but during and after his reign it blossomed with crops, sweet-smelling flowers and other plants as fruitfully as anywhere else in the world.*

What was the response of the West?

News of the fall of Edessa reached western Europe later in 1145 and caused consternation. It was the first time in the existence of the kingdom that a crusader state had been successfully invaded. Outremer was such an established part of Christian thinking that the reaction in the West was to raise large armies and go to the aid of the crusaders. This would not be an armed pilgrimage like the First Crusade, but a specifically military expedition with a strategic objective: the city of Edessa.

The papacy and the *Quantum praedecessores*

It was Pope Eugenius III who took control of the western response and issued the famous crusade bull, the *Quantum praedecessores*, in December 1145. This document set down in writing for the first time the indulgences, remission of sins and conditions of service on the crusade. It referred explicitly to the First Crusade, and linked its early great success with the new venture required now, in 1145. The document was clear evidence of the papacy regaining command of the crusading movement, following on from the papal approval of the new military orders, and it reinforced the fact that the pope was at the head of Christendom politically as well as spiritually.

In the bull, Pope Urban II was mentioned three times, the 'predecessor of happy memory'. The success of the First Crusade was a constant theme, with references to 'fathers and sons' in an effort to link past with present. The threat to the Church and to all of Christianity was presented as very grave. The message was that all the efforts of the fathers on the First Crusade would be for nothing if the sons did not answer this call to join a second crusade. Clearly, the papal propaganda machine was working overtime, as Urban had done in 1095. There was no danger to Jerusalem or to the kingdom as a whole in 1145, but the papacy was determined that war-fever needed to be whipped up and a vast army galvanised into action.

What were the privileges offered to the crusaders in 1145?

To this end, specific privileges were offered to the new crusaders. Remission of punishment for all sins was repeatedly offered, including to those who died on the journey. The Church would also offer legal protection to crusading families and their property, and interest owed on debts would be suspended. Such privileges had been on offer in 1095, but the papal bull of 1145 set them down formally in writing.

Source

 From the *Quantum praedecessores*, 1 March 1146:

We recognise how great the danger is that threatens the Church of God and all Christianity because of this [the capture of Edessa] and we do not believe that it is hidden from your understanding. It will be seen as a great token of nobility and uprightness if those things acquired by the efforts of your fathers are vigorously defended by you, their good sons. But if, God forbid, it comes to pass differently, then the bravery of the fathers will have proved to be diminished in the sons …

We, providing with a father's concern for your peace of mind and the abandonment of the eastern Church, by the authority given us by God concede and confirm to those who, inspired by devotion, decide to take up and complete so holy and very necessary a work and labour, that remission of sins which our aforesaid predecessor Pope Urban instituted. And we decree that their wives and children, goods and possessions should remain under the protection of the Holy Church; under our protection and that of the archbishops, bishops and other prelates of the Church of God. And by apostolic authority we forbid any legal suit to be brought thereafter concerning all the possessions they hold peacefully … All those who are encumbered with debts and undertake so holy a journey with pure hearts need not pay usury [interest] on past loans; and if they or others on their behalf are bound by oath of faith to usurious contracts we absolve them by apostolic authority …

ACTIVITY

Read Source E and answer the following questions.

1   How does this source make use of the earlier crusaders' achievements to encourage the second crusaders?

2   List all the things that the Pope offers to protect for the crusaders in the bull.

The preaching of the crusade

The preaching of the crusade was carefully planned to gain maximum recruitment. The bull was addressed to the king of France, Louis VII. There was a great assembly at Vézelay, France, on Easter Sunday, 31 March 1146, when the king and his nobles gathered to take the cross. It was usual to hold such meetings on saints' days and religious festivals.

Pope Eugenius entrusted the preaching of the crusade to his greatest clergyman, Bernard of Clairvaux. Bernard was a theologian, preacher and the author of the Rule for the Knights Templars (see pages 73–74). Bernard had a clear mandate; the preaching of the Second Crusade would be designed to keep the authorised preachers 'on-message'. The Pope wanted to avoid at all costs the frenzied explosion of religious passion that had been seen in 1095–96, when people such as Peter the Hermit had taken the crusade in another direction which led to the massacre of thousands of German Jews. This time, only Bernard and official preachers would recruit for the crusade. Bernard toured the Rhineland and the Low Countries for seven months. Using his famous preaching skills, he offered personal salvation, telling his listeners that they were lucky to have the opportunity to gain eternal

glory in this holy war. Bernard's mass rallies were often followed by rumours of miracles, such was the religious hysteria stirred up by his preaching. But despite the best efforts of Bernard and the Pope, an unauthorised preacher named Rudolph whipped up anti-Semitic attacks in Germany again, though the killings were not on the scale of 1096–97.

> **Source**
>
> (F)   This troubadour song was written in Old French by an unknown author around 1146–47. It is a useful secular source, telling us about the attitudes of the knightly classes towards warfare:
>
> *Anyone who now goes with Louis need have no fear of Hell, for his soul will be in Paradise with the angels of Our Lord.*
>
> *God has organised a tourney [tournament] between Heaven and Hell, and so He is asking all His friends who are willing to support His cause not to fail Him …*
>
> *For the son of God the creator has fixed a day for being at Edessa; there shall the sinners be saved … who will fight fiercely and, for the love of Him, will go and help Him in this hour of need … to wreak the vengeance of God.*

ACTIVITY

Using Source F and your own knowledge, explain why Bernard's preaching was so successful.

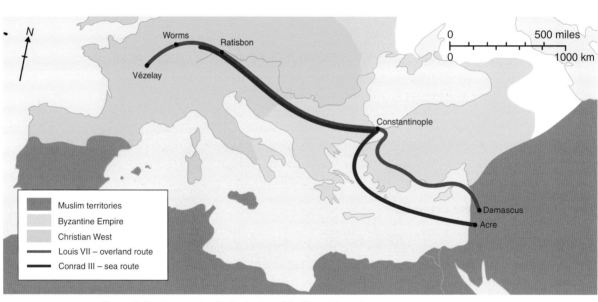

Figure 7.1   Routes taken by the leaders of the Second Crusade.

In what ways was the Second Crusade different from the First?

Since the success of the First Crusade had established a kingdom with castles garrisoned partly by new orders of warrior-monks, any new crusade from the West would be very different from the crusade of 1095. Furthermore, Europe had changed. The monastic orders were expanding, the status of the papacy was assured after the Investiture Contest (see page

12) and the capture of Jerusalem. In addition, the knightly classes were increasingly defined as an elite group by laws and taxes, and in popular culture such as poems and songs.

Who were the leaders of the Second Crusade?

King Louis VII of France

The immediate difference between the First and Second Crusades was in the leaders. King Louis VII of France announced at his Christmas court that he would help the Latin settlers in the Holy Land, but it was not until the papal bull arrived in northern France that Pope and King combined forces to launch the crusade. It was a new departure for a king to lead a crusade; especially a young king who had yet to produce a male heir. Leaving his kingdom for a distant and dangerous destination – however holy – could create a power vacuum at home to be exploited by ruthless and rebellious subjects, whatever punishment the Church threatened. Given the casualty rate of the First Crusade, it was also possible that Louis would never return.

In June 1147, in the church of St Denis in Paris, King Louis kissed the relics and begged permission to go on the crusade, in the presence of Pope Eugenius and thousands of nobles, clergy and peasants. The King took the oriflamme, France's most sacred banner – believed to have belonged to Charlemagne – and the Pope gave him his pilgrim's wallet, the symbol of his new role as a pilgrim. This great ceremony showed the world that the Pope was at the head of the crusade.

Emperor Conrad III of Germany

Conrad was an experienced crusader, having visited the Holy Land in 1123–24. Bernard of Clairvaux was keen to get the emperor involved, as it was hoped that by ensuring that the German crusaders had proper leadership, any repeat of the anti-Semitic massacres that had taken place in 1096 under Peter the Hermit would be avoided. By this time, relations between papacy and empire were much improved. This contrasted with the time of the First Crusade, when the consequences of the Investiture Contest were still being felt and both parties were licking their wounds. Now it was time for the Emperor to show that he was defender of the Church and in March 1147, Conrad established peace throughout his realm and confirmed that his son Henry would succeed him, if he should die on the crusade.

What was the response of the Byzantine Empire?

Unlike the First Crusade, where the Byzantine Emperor Alexius had specifically requested military aid, the Second Crusade was very much uninvited and was seen as a threat by the Byzantine Emperor Manuel Comnenus. He refortified the walls of Constantinople, attempted to obtain a guarantee of the crusaders' good behaviour from the Pope, and tried to persuade the crusaders to swear oaths of fealty as they had done in 1096 (see page 36). The fact that the French were on good terms with Sicily, the deadly enemy of Byzantium, made him still more uneasy. Indeed, when the French army arrived at Constantinople, a faction planned to attack the city, distrusting a treaty between the Greeks and the Seljuk Turks. The French also disliked the Byzantines because Raymond of Antioch was the French Queen Eleanor's uncle, and Byzantium had been at war with Antioch. The fact that the Second Crusade was aiming to restore Edessa, which would certainly encroach on Byzantine territory, did not encourage Emperor Manuel to support the crusaders. Finally, the long-running doctrinal differences between the Roman Catholic and Greek Orthodox Churches also played a part in the suspicions and dislike between East and West.

Sources

(G) Michael the Syrian, writing around 1150–99:

The emperor knew that having crossed over the sea and established their influence they [the crusaders] would not give it up to the empire of the Greeks and therefore he worked in concert with the Turks.

(H) The *Annals* of Niketas Choniates, written after 1204, describe the treachery of the Greeks:

When the Germans approached the gates of the cities, the citizens did not display their wares but rather let ropes down from the wall so that they could first pull up the money in payment for whatever they were hawking and then let down only as much as suited them, whether it was for bread or any other saleable foodstuff. By knowingly committing these unlawful acts, they incensed the All-Seeing Eye, for cheating at the scales and for taking no pity on them as strangers and for not even setting before them, as co-religionists, any of their own household stores …

ACTIVITY

Using Sources G and H and your own knowledge, assess the reasons for the distrust between the Byzantines and the crusaders.

Figure 7.2   Louis and Conrad set out for the Second Crusade (from a fourteenth-century manuscript).

Why did the Second Crusade fail?

Given that the Second Crusade was clearly directed by the papacy, sanctioned by the papal bull of Eugenius III and the preaching of Bernard of Clairvaux, and that it was to be led by the king of France and the German emperor, all the signs were there for a stunning success. Unfortunately, it was an embarrassing disaster.

What happened to the German contingent?

The German army marched ahead of the French army through Hungary and into Byzantine territories, where they clashed with Byzantine forces. A flash flood near Constantinople wiped out many men and much equipment, but the Emperor Manuel Comnenus reprovisioned them (he was related to Conrad through Conrad's wife, Bertha of Salzburg) and sent them on their way into Asia Minor, where they were cut to pieces by a Turkish force. Poor discipline, treachery and Conrad's own incompetence were the reasons. Conrad escaped and managed to join the advancing French army.

What successes did the French achieve?

King Louis vetoed the plan to attack the city of Constantinople, and the Emperor Manuel Comnenus was relieved to see the French army cross the Straits of the Bosphorus and enter Asia Minor. Here they learnt of the German defeat. The plan was of course to recapture the lost city of Edessa, which would involve campaigning in northern Syria. Louis led his forces towards Antioch, from where such a campaign could be directed, and in December 1147 defeated a Turkish army in the Maeander valley. This victory was dashed in January 1148 by a crushing defeat at the hands of the Turks in the Cadmus mountains. It was this defeat which broke the spirit of Louis' army. So poor was morale and so heavy the casualties, that the Templars took command of the remains of the French army and led them to Antioch in March 1148.

Figure 7.3 The Council of Jerusalem decide to attack Damascus (from a thirteenth-century manuscript).

Why didn't Louis go east to recapture Edessa?

After arriving in Antioch, Louis decided to take his army south, rather than campaign in the north to recapture Edessa. This was for several reasons:

- Louis' army had been severely depleted by the defeat in January, and he needed reinforcements from other crusaders who were coming by sea and would land further south.

- A second Muslim attack on Edessa in 1146 had destroyed most of the city, making it not worth the effort of recapture.

- Louis did not want to join forces with the crusaders of Antioch because it had been under Byzantine rule since 1145; any gains for the region would therefore go to the Emperor in Constantinople.

- Finally, and most damaging, Louis fell out with Raymond of Antioch. It was rumoured that Raymond had had an affair with Louis' wife, Queen Eleanor (his niece). This became one of the great scandals of the day, widely reported and taken quite seriously.

Why did the crusaders attack Damascus?

The crusaders had two alternatives. They could try to capture the only Muslim-held port of Ascalon, or they could attack Damascus, the major Muslim power close to Jerusalem, which would also put an end to any possible alliance between Nur ad-Din's Aleppo and Damascus.

The decision was made to besiege Damascus, and the attack began in July 1148. However, it lasted only three days before the crusade army withdrew because of lack of water. The Second Crusade had come to an ignominious end.

Sources

I **A letter from Emperor Conrad to the Abbot of Corvey, 1148:**

When following the advice of the common council we had gone to Damascus and after a great deal of trouble had pitched our camps before the gate of the city, it was certainly near being taken. But certain ones, whom we least suspected, treasonably asserted that the city was impregnable on that side and hastily led us to another position where no water could be supplied for the troops and where access was impossible to anyone. And thus all, equally indignant grieved, returned, leaving the undertaking uncompleted.

J **From William of Tyre (writing around the 1170s):**

The city, as we have said, was in despair and its citizens held no hope of resisting or of being saved, but rather they were packing their bags and preparing to leave. At this point, for our sins, they began to work on the greed of our men. With consummate skill they proposed a variety of arguments to some of our princes and they promised and delivered a stupendous sum of money to them so that the princes would strive and labour to lift the siege. By impious suggestions they persuaded the kings and the leaders of the pilgrims, who trusted their good faith and industry, to leave the orchards and to lead the army to the opposite side of the city. The kings and all the leaders of the army believed them and they deserted the places which they had earlier won with so much sweat and at the cost of the lives of so many of their men. They transferred all of their formations and, under the leadership of the traitors, they camped on the opposite side of the city. There they found themselves located far from access to water, deprived of the abundance of fruit, and lacking almost all supplies. They were saddened and they discovered, all too late, that they had maliciously been led to move from a region of abundance.

ACTIVITY

Using Sources I and J and your own knowledge, explain why the crusaders failed to capture Damascus.

Who was to blame for the failure of the Second Crusade?

After such great expense and high hopes from the leading king in Europe and the German emperor, the collapse of the Second Crusade created a good deal of bitterness both in Europe and in Outremer. Many possibilities were put forward, none of them certain. Emperor Conrad thought that the settlers had been bribed by the Muslims in Damascus, others thought that Raymond of Antioch had interfered, or that the local nobility resented the outsiders taking any plunder. The Templars and Hospitallers were also blamed, and the Greeks too, for treachery. Whatever the reason, it was Bernard of Clairvaux who took the fullest share of the blame, for it was he who had preached the crusade and had to justify why it had failed so spectacularly. Bernard remained defiant, however, telling the crusaders and the Christian world to look to their own conscience to find an answer.

Sources

 K   **An anonymous chronicler from Wurzburg, writing in 1147:**

God allowed the Western church, on account of its sins, to be cast down. There arose, indeed, certain pseudo-prophets, sons of Belial, and witnesses of anti-Christ, who seduced the Christians with empty words. They constrained all sorts of men, by vain preaching, to set out against the Saracens in order to liberate Jerusalem. The preaching of these men was so enormously influential that the inhabitants of nearly every region, by common vows, offered themselves freely for common destruction. Not only the ordinary people, but kings, dukes, marquises, and other powerful men of this world as well, believed that they thus showed their allegiance to God. The bishops, archbishops, abbots, and other ministers and prelates of the church joined in this error, throwing themselves headlong into it to the great peril of bodies and souls ...

L   **From Bernard of Clairvaux's** *Apology***:**

These few things have been said by way of apology, so that your conscience may have something from me, whereby you can hold yourself and me excused, if not in the eyes of those who judge causes from their results, then at least in your own eyes. The perfect and final apology for any man is the testimony of his own conscience. As for myself, I take it to be a small matter to be judged by those 'who call evil good, and good evil, whose darkness is light, whose light darkness.'

If one or the other must be done, I would rather that men murmur against us than against God. It would be well for me if he deigns to use me for his shield ... I shall not refuse to be made ignominious, so long as God's glory is not attacked.

The failure of the Second Crusade was not just a blow to the pride of the West, it also left the Holy Land exposed and demoralised. Nur ad-Din, Zengi's son, defeated Prince Raymond of Antioch at the Battle of Inab in June 1149, sending the prince's head to the Caliph of Baghdad. King Baldwin III marched north to restore order, appealing to the West for aid and selling castles in the county of Edessa to the Byzantines. No help came from the West, despite meetings between Bernard of Clairvaux and Pope Eugenius, and this final failure formed a miserable epilogue to the Second Crusade.

ACTIVITY

Read Sources K and L and compare them as evidence for the failure of the Second Crusade.

Conclusion

The failure of the Second Crusade was far-reaching:

- Many western Europeans were turned against the whole idea of crusading.

- The papacy lost a great deal of prestige.

- The Second Crusade was the last crusade in which the armies were accompanied by large groups of pilgrims, young, old and sick, in the tradition of the 1095 crusade.

- The crusades now became strictly military expeditions, whose objectives were limited, military ones.

- Relationships between Byzantium and the crusaders deteriorated further.

- The princes of the West and the settlers in the Latin states in the East had very little trust and respect for one another from now on.

- Most important of all was the effect of the Second Crusade on the Muslims. The bold move by Zengi showed the world that Islamic armies could capture and hold Christian territory. The failure of the crusade to achieve any victories whatever in the East from 1146–48 destroyed the reputation of western military strength. It was partly responsible for causing the Muslim states of the East to draw closer together and to unite for further attacks upon the Latin states. This encouraged the jihad and sowed the seeds for the ultimate downfall of the kingdom in 1187.

Review questions

1   To what extent were divisions within the Christian community in the Holy Land responsible for the fall of Edessa?

2   How extensive was the appeal of the Second Crusade?

3   To what extent did the Second Crusade differ from the First Crusade?

4   How significant was the lack of Byzantine support in bringing about the failure of the Second Crusade?

5   To what extent were the rulers of France and Germany responsible for the failure of the Second Crusade?

How did the Muslim world change in response to the crusader kingdom?

8

Key Questions:

In this chapter you will learn:

- How the Muslim world began to unite
- Why Nur ad-Din was important
- How Saladin grew powerful enough to seriously threaten the crusader kingdom
- Why relations between Christians and Muslims changed

You will also develop the following skills:

- Assessing the language and tone of documents
- Comparing sources and their limitations
- Analysing the impact of individuals
- Making a judgement on the long-term development of Muslim unity

Introduction

The population of the Near East was extremely diverse and the Muslim world in the early twelfth century was divided into tribes and kingdoms that were split between the Sunni and Shia orthodoxies (see page 41). The First Crusade had succeeded in achieving its objectives, and it had been possible to found Latin states in the East largely because the Muslims had been divided against one another and had thus been unable to cooperate effectively to stave off their western foes. The end of the Second Crusade saw the Muslims preparing to unite, for the first time, against the Latin intruders in their midst, while the Latins, for their part, were sharply divided against one another. It was chiefly Zengi and Nur ad-Din, atabegs of Mosul, who spearheaded the Arab counter-attack against the West in the period 1130–75. The greatest Muslim leader of them all was Saladin. A profoundly orthodox Kurd, he brought Egypt back and gave the Muslim world a new prestige in the 1180s which was to challenge and then virtually destroy the crusader kingdom in 1187.

The growing unity of the Muslim world during the twelfth century was a factor which brought about the downfall of the crusader kingdom in 1187. In 1095 the Arab world was not a combined community. It was a myriad of tribal and racial components, from the Seljuks in Asia Minor to the Fatimids in Egypt and the Sultan in Baghdad, based in the regional centres of Aleppo, Damascus and Cairo. Whenever the Muslims brought a sizeable army to the battlefield, they could and did gain the victory, as at the Field of Blood in 1119 and the Battle of Inab in 1149. However, until the Muslim world was united under one leader with a coherent strategy commanding respect, any victory would be unsustainable. That leader was Saladin, but he himself built on the considerable achievements of Nur ad-Din, Zengi's son.

Source

 William of Tyre, writing in the 1170s, on the rising Muslim unity:

Within quite recent times, Zengi ... first conquered many other kingdoms by force and then laid violent hands on Edessa ... then his son, Nur ad-Din, drove the king of Damascus from his own land and seized the ancient and wealthy kingdom of Egypt as his own. ... this Saladin, a man of humble antecedents and lowly station, now holds under his control all these kingdoms. From Egypt and the countries adjacent to it, he draws an inestimable supply of the purest gold ... other provinces furnish him numberless companies of horsemen and fighters ...

Arab writers of the twelfth and thirteenth centuries

Kamal ad-Din was based in Aleppo. Writing in the thirteenth century, he provided important material on events in northern Syria.

Ibn al-Athir wrote a history of the Muslim world and was an eyewitness of Saladin's career, writing with a personal but well resourced view.

Baha ad-Din wrote a biography of Saladin, having served with him and admired him greatly.

Imad ad-Din was secretary first to Nur ad-Din and then to Saladin. Chancellor and a scholar, he wrote a history of the fall of Jerusalem.

Usama ibn Munqidh was the emir of Shaizir. His life spanned most of the twelfth century, and his autobiography is full of anecdotes and references which provide a fascinating insight to the Holy Land in peace and in war.

KEY ISSUES

- What were the achievements of Nur ad-Din?
- How far was Saladin able to unite the Muslim world from 1174 to 1187?
- How did attitudes between East and West change in the period 1146–92?

Chapter timeline

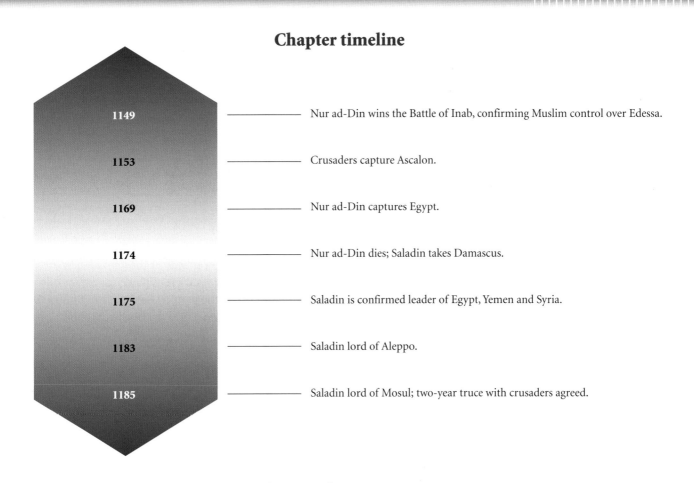

1149	Nur ad-Din wins the Battle of Inab, confirming Muslim control over Edessa.
1153	Crusaders capture Ascalon.
1169	Nur ad-Din captures Egypt.
1174	Nur ad-Din dies; Saladin takes Damascus.
1175	Saladin is confirmed leader of Egypt, Yemen and Syria.
1183	Saladin lord of Aleppo.
1185	Saladin lord of Mosul; two-year truce with crusaders agreed.

What were the achievements of Nur ad-Din?

How did Nur ad-Din develop the notion of the *jihad*?

Zengi's son, Nur ad-Din, was a different character altogether from his father. His pious reputation as the just, puritanical *mujahid* (religious warrior) was displayed in inscriptions on coins, in his patronage of religious learning, schools, scholars and mosques. New religious schools (madrasas) grew throughout Syria; Nur ad-Din founded twenty or so of the forty that were built during his reign. He cultivated the image of the just ruler: judge, jurist and theologian, educated, literate and orthodox, but he was not a fanatic. His piety increased after illnesses in 1157 and 1159 and defeats in 1163.

In 1161 he took the **hajj** and rebuilt the walls of the city of Medina, a political as well as holy act, declaring his new power in Islam. The inscription on the *minbar* (pulpit) of the mosque in Aleppo declared his intention to relocate it to the al-Aqsa mosque in Jerusalem when the Holy City (*al Quds* to the Arabs) had been recaptured. This was a statement of political and spiritual ambition.

Nur ad-Din was forced to concentrate on resources in Syria so that he could consolidate his power before extending it. The jihad was integrated into Nur ad-Din's policies, as he regularly demanded support for renewals of the holy war. Religious propagandists travelled in his armies. Nur ad-Din was careful to offer unity under the nominal authority of the Sunni caliph of Baghdad, whose permission was sought for each conquest and annexation.

hajj
The pilgrimage to Mecca, in Arabia. Mecca is important to Muslims as the town where Muhammad proclaimed the new Islamic religion. Every able-bodied Muslim who can afford it must complete this journey at least once in their lifetime.

> **Source**
>
> **(B)** Ibn al-Athir, writing in the early thirteenth century, describes the character of Nur ad-Din:
>
> *Among his virtues were austerity, piety and a knowledge of theology. His food and clothing and all his personal expenditure came out of income from properties bought with his legal share of booty and money allocated for communal Muslims' interests. He often got up to pray at night, and his vigils and meditations inspired praise.*

By the time of his death in 1174, Nur ad-Din had confirmed and further raised the profile of the jihad as a real concept of political and military power against the Christian West. His death came at a crucial time for both religions, for King Baldwin, a powerful enemy, also died that year. But whereas Baldwin was succeeded by the leprous Baldwin IV, Nur ad-Din was succeeded by the one man who launched the Muslim world decisively onto the increasingly fragile and enfeebled Christian kingdom: Saladin.

What were the military achievements of Nur ad-Din?

Nur ad-Din's victory against Prince Raymond of Antioch at the Battle of Inab in 1149 confirmed the Muslim hold over Edessa and the surrounding region, but it was not until the 1160s that Nur ad-Din began to threaten the crusader kingdom with any seriousness. His main rival was King Amalric and the theatre of conflict was Egypt. Until Nur ad-Din's death in 1174, battles and campaigns raged continually, prompting Amalric's appeals to the West. For the first time since 1100, Outremer faced real opposition on all fronts.

The struggle for Egypt

Egypt was attractive for the following reasons:

- The Shia Fatimid dynasty was in decline, and had lost Jerusalem in 1099 and Ascalon in 1153 to the crusaders.
- Egypt was wealthy and would pay for troops and provide food for whoever governed it; Alexandria, on Egypt's north coast, was the prime port of the eastern Mediterranean.
- If the crusaders did not conquer Egypt then Nur ad-Din would, uniting for the first time Shia Muslims with the Sunni in Syria and therefore encircling the Christian kingdom.

King Amalric was Nur ad-Din's main rival. From 1163 to 1169, he led five campaigns into Egypt, or Babylon, as the crusaders called it, but without success. The problem was that when he was invading Egypt, Nur ad-Din could attack Outremer in the north, which happened in 1164 when Amalric attacked Bilbais, north-east of Cairo; Nur ad-Din took the towns of Harim and Banyas from Antioch and took the kingdom itself in 1164.

In 1167 Nur-ad-Din's general, **Shirkuh**, led an assault on Egypt. This prompted an Egyptian–Christian alliance. The Shia caliphate in Cairo was so desperate to fend off Shirkuh's Sunni invasion that it paid the Christians 400,000 dinars to remain in Egypt until the threat from Nur ad-Din's army had subsided.

> **BIOGRAPHY**
>
> **Shirkuh (died 1169)**
>
> A Kurdish nobleman and warrior from Baghdad and Tikrit. He served under Zengi and then under Nur ad-Din, with great effect. He became chief general in Egypt and eventually vizier.

The conquest of Egypt

The two armies clashed in battle at Beben, south of Cairo. Neither had the decisive victory, but Shirkuh managed to capture Alexandria. Amalric laid siege to the city and it fell to the crusaders later in 1167; a truce was arranged and both armies left Egypt.

The prestige of the crusader army had been restored after the disastrous Second Crusade. A Christian army had captured a major Islamic city, the appeals to the West were bringing in recruits – though not many – and relations with Byzantium were stronger than ever when Amalric married the niece of the Byzantine Emperor Manuel that year.

In 1168 Amalric invaded Egypt again, but this time he was outmanoeuvred by Shirkuh. When the caliph was assassinated in January 1169, Egypt fell to Nur ad-Din's army. This was a major blow to the crusader kingdom. Its true consequences were to be realised in 1187 when Shirkuh's nephew, Saladin, had all the resources of Egypt at his disposal to enable him to invade Outremer when it was at its weakest. It also meant that future crusades from the West would have to invade or at least confront the problem of the Egyptian resources, which were now in the hands of the Sunni Muslims. From 1169 onwards, appeals to the West – and to Byzantium – for men and money grew increasingly urgent, for good reason.

> **Source**
>
> **From William of Tyre, writing in the 1170s:**
>
> *[Nur ad-Din] could effectively shut in the realm and blockade all coastal cities by land and sea … still more to be dreaded was the fact that he could hinder the passage of pilgrims on their way to us …*

The deaths of Nur ad-Din and King Amalric

Undeterred, Amalric set about planning another invasion of Egypt. He was encouraged by the dissent within Egypt brought about by Saladin, who had deposed the Shia caliph in 1171 and refused to join Nur ad-Din to fight the crusaders in 1173. In May 1174 Nur ad-Din died from a heart attack, leaving Syria leaderless and Egypt unstable. Amalric had secured naval support from the Sicilians, who put a fleet to sea. Everything looked good for a successful invasion of Egypt, but in July 1174 Amalric himself died from dysentery, aged only 38. His successor was Baldwin IV, a thirteen-year-old boy with leprosy.

> ***ACTIVITY***
>
> Why was Egypt so important to the Christians and the Muslims?

How far was Saladin able to unite the Muslim world from 1174 to 1187?

In 1174, both Christian and Muslim worlds were in a state of flux and potential disarray. It was Saladin who regrouped and energised Islam faster and more effectively than the Christians, with their divided nobility and enfeebled resources, could mobilise. But Saladin was not the son of Nur ad-Din. His father was Shirkuh, who had consolidated his grip on Egypt in the years 1169–74 and in 1174 took control of Damascus. Saladin's policy of championing the Sunni orthodoxy gave him the respectability he needed, and in 1175 the Caliph of Baghdad invested him with the government of Egypt, Yemen and Syria. In 1176 he married Nur ad-Din's widow, thereby enforcing his image as the spiritual successor to Nur ad-Din.

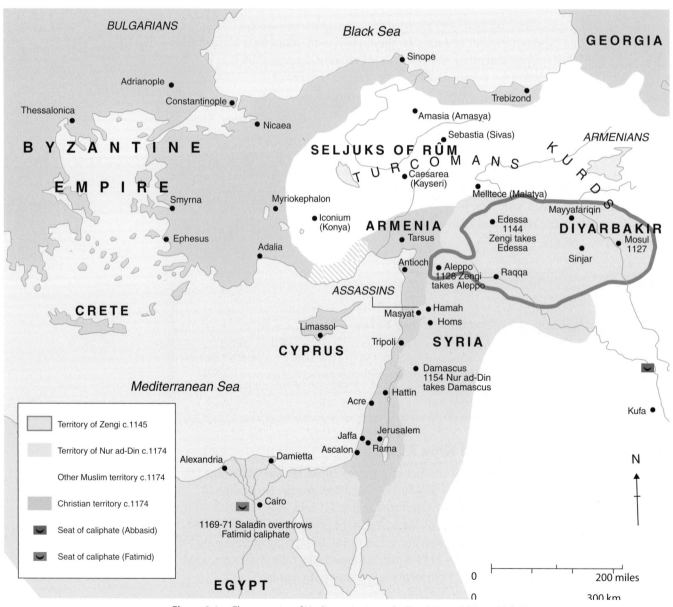

Figure 8.1 The expansion of Muslim territories under Zengi, Nur-ad-Din and Saladin, 1144–74.

How did Saladin restore Muslim unity?

Saladin rose to power first by defying Nur ad-Din and then by assuming Nur ad-Din's status as leader of the jihad. As the son of a Kurdish mercenary in the service of Zengi of Mosul, Saladin was an upstart who needed the legitimacy that the jihad could bestow. He was ruling a Turkish military elite and he had to be the orthodox leader, whether out of private conviction or public convenience. Public displays of religious devotion and personal piety were prominent features in his style as ruler, the ritual cleansing of the Dome of the Rock performed in person, the moving of the *minbar* from Aleppo, gaining formal recognition from the caliphs of Baghdad.

Saladin was not without Muslim enemies, however. As guardian of the Sunni orthodoxy, he was the target of two assassination attempts by the Shia **Assassins** in 1175. In response, he sent troops to the Assassins' castle at Masyaf and ravaged the area, but from then on he only ever slept in a wooden tower for protection.

Figure 8.2   Saladin.

8 How did the Muslim world change in response to the crusader kingdom?

Assassins

The Assassins, as they were known at the time, were a Shia sect of Muslims. They were based in castles in the mountains of northern Syria, where most Muslims were Sunni. Their name derived from their use of hashish, which gave their killers a trancelike fanaticism under the leadership of the 'Old Man of the Mountains'. Even within the Shia Muslims, they were a feared splinter group who murdered Christians and Muslims alike. King Amalric approached them for an alliance in 1171. In 1175 they attempted to assassinate Saladin, who was the Sunni champion. Saladin's cheek was slashed and his chest armour pierced, but he survived, though for the rest of his life he only ever slept in a wooden tower, such was his fear of future assassination.

Saladin's role sat uneasily with the Seljuk Turks in Anatolia and with the Seljuks of Iran, and he was never warmly received by the caliphs of Baghdad. He was seen as a threat by many as he expanded outwards from his base in Egypt into Syria; his use of the jihad was viewed by some as a tool to further his political and military ends, and his truces with the crusaders were opportunities for him to deal with his co-religionist rivalries. Certainly the western Christians in Outremer and the eastern Christians in Byzantium were in doubt as to Saladin's territorial ambitions, hence their repeated appeals to the West.

Source

(D) **Baha ad-Din, writing in the early thirteenth century, describes the character of Saladin:**

The Holy War and the suffering involved in it weighed heavily on his heart and his whole being in every limb; he spoke of nothing else, thought about equipment for the fight, was interested only in those who had taken up arms, had little sympathy with anyone who spoke of anything else or encouraged any other activity. For love of the Holy War and on God's path he left his family and his sons, his homeland, his house and all his estates, and chose out of all the world to live in the shade of his tent, where the winds blew on him from every side ...'

The Battle of Montgisard

The crusader kingdom planned another invasion of Egypt in 1177, involving forces from Outremer, Byzantium and Philip of Flanders' troops. Nothing came of it, however, because the participants could not agree who would rule Egypt once it was conquered. At this time Saladin was not yet strong enough to comprehensively defeat the united Christian forces, so a great opportunity was missed. Instead, Saladin attacked the kingdom but was caught by surprise at Montgisard, near Ibelin, by a crusader army led by Baldwin IV. He narrowly escaped. Hundreds were killed on both sides, but Saladin certainly came off worse. The battle proved that Saladin was not that powerful, even with the combined forces of Egypt and Syria behind him.

The castle at Jacob's Ford

In 1178 the crusaders built a castle at Jacob's Ford, on the River Jordan, only 30 miles from Damascus, a direct threat to Damascus and a highly aggressive act. The planning and building were partly supervised by King Baldwin IV. The castle was expansive and well built and would house 80 Templars and 900 footsoldiers. Saladin offered to buy off the crusaders with 100,000 dinars, but was turned down. However, in August 1179 Saladin marched on the castle and captured it in five days; it was probably unfinished, but this did not help the garrison. The Templars and archers were all executed. It was a severe blow to the crusader kingdom, but fortunately for them Saladin could not follow up this success because of an epidemic in his army and a drought in Syria.

Saladin takes Mosul and Aleppo

Powerful though he undoubtedly was in 1180, Saladin was still not the supreme leader of Islam he needed to be in order to destroy Outremer once and for all. A truce with the kingdom was arranged for two years from 1180 to 1182, and in the summer of 1182 Saladin's forces were defeated in southern Galilee and his blockade of the port of Beirut thwarted. However, the death of Nur ad-Din's son, as-Salih, ruler of Mosul, gave Saladin the opportunity he needed to march into the town. In 1183 he forced Aleppo to surrender to him. Saladin could now say that he was truly the rightful champion of Islam and the one person who could defeat the Christian kingdom. Earlier in 1183 he had captured crusaders who had launched a daring raid in the Red Sea and killed many Muslim merchants and pilgrims at sea and on land. Saladin hit back hard, executing the Christians in towns and villages across his lands, and taking two captives to Mecca where they were executed in front of massed pilgrims. By 1185 Saladin had forced Mosul to recognise him as overlord and his prestige was at its height – just as the kingdom of Jerusalem was about to plunge into dissent, dispute and total division.

How did attitudes between East and West change in the period 1119–92?

During the early years of the crusader kingdom the westerners were in a tiny minority; despite the slaughter of those in Jerusalem in 1099, the Christians could not be at war continuously with the Muslims. The crusaders in the early decades of the new kingdom often established alliances with Muslim factions; they needed the military and economic support of the indigenous populations and could not afford to overtax or treat them harshly for fear of rebellion.

> ### Source
>
> (E)   **Usama ibn Munqidh, writing in the twelfth century, describes his experience of Christian–Muslim relations:**
>
> *There are some Franks who have settled in our land and taken to living like Muslims. A very important Frankish knight was staying in the camp of King Fulk, the son of Fulk. He had come on a pilgrimage and was going home again. We got to know one another, and became firm friends. He called me 'brother' and an affectionate friendship grew up between us.*

ACTIVITY

How far was the Muslim conquest of Egypt the **main** reason for Saladin's rise to power?

You could include the following reasons in your answer before making a judgement on the main reason:

- the achievements of Nur-ad-Din 1148–74
- the growing movement of the jihad in the Arab world
- the increasing weakness in the Christian kingdom
- the conquest of Egypt itself.

P

8 How did the Muslim world change in response to the crusader kingdom?

The defeat at the Battle of the Field of Blood in 1119, where Prince Roger of Antioch and large numbers of the Antioch nobility were killed, was something of a turning point. The church council at Nablus in 1120 forbade sexual relations between Muslims and Christians (see pages 58–59). The severity of the punishments imposed certainly suggests that people were conducting sexual relations across the religious divide.

Attitudes after the Second Crusade (1146–49) continued to harden. While it used to be thought that the western settlers adapted to the eastern way of life, they probably remained more aloof and segregated, inhabiting only certain areas. Even so, they farmed the countryside and lived in houses in villages rather than purely behind the defensive gates of the castles, especially in the first half of the twelfth century.

Sources

F Imad ad-Din, writing in the 1190s, describes the licentiousness of western women:

There arrived by ship three hundred lovely Frankish women, full of youth and beauty, assembled from beyond the sea and offering themselves for sin. They dedicated as a holy offering what they kept between their thighs; they were openly licentious and devoted themselves to relaxation; they removed every obstacle to making of themselves free offerings. They interwove leg with leg, slaked their lovers' thirsts, caught lizard after lizard in their holes, guided pens to inkwells, torrents to the valley bottom, streams to pools, swords to scabbards, gold ingots to crucibles ...

G Ibn Jubayr was a Spanish Muslim from Granada. This account, written in 1184, reveals how far the Christian and Muslim co-existence had developed by then:

One of the astonishing things that is talked of is that although the fires of discord burn between the two parties, Muslim and Christian, two armies of them may meet and dispose themselves in battle array, and yet Muslim and Christian travellers will come and go between them without interference. The Christians impose a tax on the Muslims in their land which gives them full security; and likewise the Christian merchants pay a tax upon their goods in Muslim lands. Agreement exists between them, and there is equal treatment in all cases. ... Our way lay through continuous farms and ordered settlements, whose inhabitants were all Muslims, living comfortably with the Franks. God protect us from such temptation. They surrender half their crops to the Franks at harvest time and pay as well a poll-tax of one dinar and five qirat for each person. Other than that, they are not interfered with, save for a light tax on the fruits of trees. Their houses and all their effects are left to their full possession.

ACTIVITY

Read Sources F and G, and answer the following questions.

1   In what ways is the author of Source F disapproving of western women?

2   Why did Christians and Muslims manage to maintain peaceful commercial relations, according to Source G?

Conclusion

It is clear that the jihad was provoked by the seizure of Jerusalem and the creation of the Kingdom of Jerusalem after 1100. Gradually, the Arab world fought back, but it was not until the leadership of Nur ad-Din and Saladin – helped by the increasing weakness of the crusader kingdom – that the dreams of restoring Jerusalem to the Muslim world were realised. Jihad became a political and military tool, skilfully used by both leaders to create a semblance of unity at least in the Holy Land, if not in the wider Arab world. Nur ad-Din achieved a great deal, laying the foundations for the ultimate success of Saladin, who used the jihad and his vast resources to attack and to destroy the crusader kingdom when it was at its weakest in 1187, to which we now turn.

Review questions

1 How successful was Nur ad-Din in uniting the Muslims?

2 To what extent did Saladin exploit the jihad to gain military ends?

3 Using Sources A to G and your own knowledge, what evidence is there of tolerance between the two religions?

9   How far was the fall of Jerusalem inevitable?

> **Key Questions:**
>
> In this chapter you will learn:
>
> - Why the West failed to send support
> - How the kingdom was internally weakened before 1187
> - How Saladin was able to comprehensively defeat the crusaders and capture Jerusalem
>
> You will also develop the following skills:
>
> - Assessing the language and tone of documents
> - Comparing sources and their limitations
> - Analysing the impact of the long-and short-term weaknesses within the kingdom
> - Making a judgement on the causes of the kingdom's collapse

Introduction

In July 1187, the Muslim leader, Saladin, wiped out the entire crusader army at the Battle of Hattin, in Syria. In a single day, castles were captured; their garrisons and the household troops of the king, as well as the military orders, were killed, captured or imprisoned. The crusader kingdom of Outremer was utterly defenceless. Weeks later, after the fall of numerous ports and castles, the Holy City of Jerusalem surrendered to the Islamic forces, never again to return to crusader control.

The failure of the Second Crusade in 1148 had indeed dealt a blow to crusader prestige and to western enthusiasm, but the fall of the kingdom was by no means apparent at that stage. It took a series of long-term causes combined with short-term events and situations to precipitate the collapse in the summer of 1187:

- The deaths of Baldwin IV and Baldwin V leaving female heirs in 1185–86.
- The coronation of Guy of Lusignan, an unpopular outsider, in 1186.
- The lack of support from the West between 1148 and 1187.
- The end of the alliance with Byzantium in 1184.
- The rise of Saladin and his domination of the Levant, from 1174 to 1187.
- The treacherous behaviour of some leading nobles, notably Reynald of Chatillon in 1187.

> **KEY ISSUES**
>
> - Why did the West fail to send reinforcements?
> - How far was the kingdom internally weakened in the period 1148–87?
> - How did the crisis of 1187 occur?
> - What happened at the Battle of Hattin?

Chapter timeline

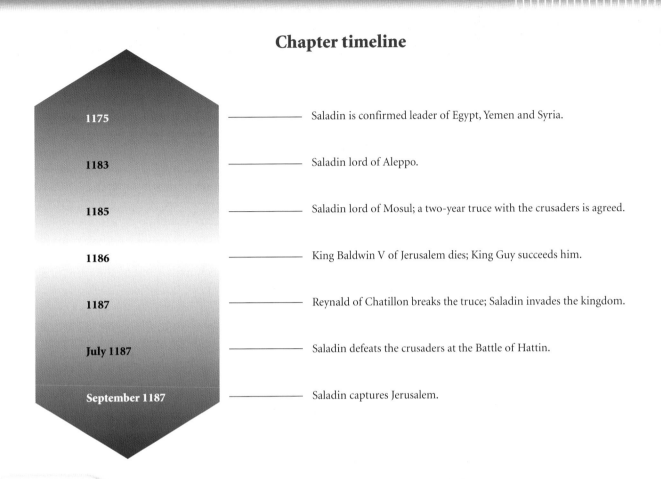

1175	Saladin is confirmed leader of Egypt, Yemen and Syria.
1183	Saladin lord of Aleppo.
1185	Saladin lord of Mosul; a two-year truce with the crusaders is agreed.
1186	King Baldwin V of Jerusalem dies; King Guy succeeds him.
1187	Reynald of Chatillon breaks the truce; Saladin invades the kingdom.
July 1187	Saladin defeats the crusaders at the Battle of Hattin.
September 1187	Saladin captures Jerusalem.

Causation

Causation is a key historical concept. This chapter is concerned with the reasons why Jerusalem and the crusader kingdom were conquered so quickly by Saladin in 1187. In examining any historical event – wars, inventions or revolutions, for example – historians need to assess the long-term causes, which extend over several decades, as well as the short-term 'triggers' which add the final spark. From your reading of the introduction and the key questions, you should now be able to draw up a table with 'long-term' and 'short-term' factors in separate columns.

Why did the West fail to send reinforcements?

The internal divisions of the kingdom were at their very worst in 1186, but it took three external factors to bring down the kingdom. The first of these was the lack of warriors from the West to defend the kingdom. This was not for want of requests from the kingdom over the decades, though political divisions in Europe kept the leaders at home.

The appeal of Gilbert d'Assailly (1166)

Pope Alexander III issued two papal bulls calling for a new crusade, the second following the appeal by the Master of the Hospitallers, Gilbert d'Assailly. Gilbert took the bull to the king of France, Louis VII (the same Louis who had failed on the Second Crusade) and to Henry II of England, who ruled Normandy and the whole of western France. (Henry had married Louis' first wife, Eleanor of Aquitaine, thereby gaining the rich duchy of Aquitaine

in south-west France.) The two kings distrusted one another, but raised taxes for the Holy Land. Several leading nobles answered the call, but kings were needed to mobilise the large armies required in Outremer.

The appeal of Archbishop Frederick of Tyre (1169)

In 1169, the growing power of Nur ad-Din (see pages 95–96) forced the crusaders to send to the West for help. They chose their most senior churchman, Archbishop Frederick of Tyre, to do this. Frederick visited the pope, bringing with him letters for the rulers of western Europe. He stressed the need for the protection of pilgrims and the seriousness of the threat to Outremer now that Egypt and Syria were united. As a result, Pope Alexander issued another bull. Frederick appealed chiefly to Henry II and Louis VII. Eleven letters had already been sent to Louis in the years 1163–65, but Louis was still haunted by his failure on the Second Crusade in 1147–48 and felt threatened by Henry II of England. This time, Frederick offered the French king the keys to Jerusalem itself, echoing the event of 800 when the Emperor Charlemagne had been given the keys. Louis, like Charlemagne, wanted to be seen as the greatest Christian ruler of Europe and defender of the Church; indeed, Charlemagne's banner, the oriflamme, was kept in the church of St Denis in Paris. But Louis could not leave the kingdom when the rivalry with the king of England was so great.

Why didn't Henry II go to the Holy Land?

Henry II had good crusader credentials in his family: his uncle was King **Amalric** and his grandfather was King Fulk. However, in 1169 Henry was embroiled in a dispute with the Archbishop of Canterbury, Thomas Becket. Peace was made between Henry II and Louis VII and between Henry II and Becket in 1170, and Frederick of Tyre was present at the settlement. But in December 1170, just as peace was within reach and the West could finally be sufficiently united to send a great army to the aid of the crusader kingdom, Becket was murdered by Henry II's knights. The King of England was condemned and there ended the feeling of goodwill and unity. Frederick returned to Outremer alone.

It took a couple of years before Henry II turned his thoughts to the East again. It was the penance imposed on Henry for the murder of Becket which worked in favour of the Holy Land: the Pope ordered Henry to provide 200 knights a year to serve with the Templars. Henry also sent 2000 silver marks to the kingdom and swore to take the cross for three years by 1173. Again, difficulties arose, this time Henry's aid to Outremer was postponed because of a rebellion led by Henry's eldest son, Henry the Younger, in 1174. (The rebellion was supported by his brothers and Henry II's wife, Eleanor, and encouraged by King Louis of France.) Henry II wrote personally to King Amalric, explaining why he could not come, evidence of his sincerity. He quashed the family rebellion, his son died of dysentery and Eleanor was kept under house-arrest until Henry's death in 1189.

BIOGRAPHY

Amalric

King of Jerusalem 1163–74. Amalric was described as strong and intelligent but very fat, apparently having breasts hanging down to his waist. He led five campaigns into Egypt and dominated the nobles. His early death at the age of 38 was a serious blow to the kingdom at precisely the time when Saladin was on the rise.

The appeal of 1181

The debilitating illness of the young King Baldwin IV (he suffered from leprosy) and the growing power of Saladin forced another appeal to Pope Alexander III, who issued another crusade appeal to the kings of France and England. The Pope was aware of Baldwin's leprosy – which he (not very helpfully) saw as God's judgement on the sins of the settlers, but once again, political issues kept the kings at home. Henry II was not the closest male relative to the dying Baldwin and he feared that if he went to the Holy Land, he would have to remain there for years. Philip of France, the young and ambitious son of Louis VII, was busy scheming to regain the territories in France which he saw as rightfully his, allying with Henry's sons against the ageing king of England. Once again, nothing was done to help the Holy Land.

The mission of Patriarch Heraclius (1184)

The combined difficulties of the threat from Saladin (see pages 99–100), the worsening illness of the young King Baldwin and the collapse of relations with Byzantium forced another appeal to the West. This appeal was at the highest level, being led by Patriarch Heraclius of Jerusalem, and the masters of both the Templars and the Hospitallars – an unprecedented mission. They met the Pope, who issued another crusade bull. They then travelled to Paris and again offered the keys to Jerusalem to the the young King Philip, but he was not sufficiently well established on the throne to accept. Heraclius turned to Henry II of England, who offered men and money but was advised by his nobles to remain in his own lands, so Heraclius returned to Outremer without a great army from the West, despite his efforts.

How far was the kingdom internally weakened in the period 1174–87?

The problem with the fall of Jerusalem is that the spectacular collapse of the kingdom in 1187 casts a long shadow of hindsight but does not necessarily mean that it was inevitable. The fall of Edessa and the failure of the Second Crusade were a blow for western prestige, but the kingdom remained strong, albeit without Edessa. Baldwin III reigned from 1143 to 1163, but he died childless and another dispute arose over the succession of Amalric. This was quickly resolved and Amalric ruled until 1174 when his son, Baldwin IV, succeeded peacefully and without any internal dispute. It was only in the years 1183–87 that internal divisions became a real issue, at precisely the time when the Arab world under Saladin was at its most united.

The issue of the leper-king

Although this succession was peaceful there were two problems; Baldwin was only thirteen and therefore was not old enough to rule by himself, so a regent had to be appointed. More seriously, Baldwin had contracted leprosy at a young age. Leprosy is a bacterial disease causing inflammation and damage to the nerves and skin. Baldwin's leprosy worsened during his teens, and he lost his sight and his nose as the bacteria multiplied. During an age when a king had to be fit and healthy to lead his armies into battle and to dominate his nobles in the council chamber, Baldwin was going to be in no state to govern the Holy Land. But his inability to lead and to control the kingdom would not necessarily mean the downfall of the kingdom. It took other factors, both internal and external, to do that. In the short term, a smooth succession had to be organised and there was every possibility that continuity and security would be assured.

The first regency and succession

Miles of Plancy, Amalric's seneschal, controlled the kingdom immediately after the coronation of Baldwin IV in 1174, but he was murdered within months. His successor was Count Raymond III of Tripoli, Baldwin's closest relative, who had spent the years 1164–74 in Muslim captivity. Raymond was an intelligent and widely respected man, and some people saw him as a potential king, though he never made a claim on the throne.

> ### Source
>
>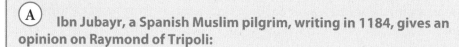
>
> **(A)** **Ibn Jubayr, a Spanish Muslim pilgrim, writing in 1184, gives an opinion on Raymond of Tripoli:**
>
> *The most considerable among the accursed Franks is the accursed count [Raymond]… He has authority and position among them. He is qualified to be king and indeed is a candidate for the office.*

Whoever married Baldwin IV's sister, Sibylla, would become king. In 1176 Raymond and the nobles had asked William Longsword to marry her. He was the son of the Count of Montferrat (in Italy) and first cousin to both French and German royal families. He accepted and married Sibylla in October 1176, so at least the succession was secured when Baldwin became too disabled to rule directly. That year King Baldwin ended his minority, aged fifteen; Raymond's regency therefore came to an end and he returned to Tripoli.

The death of William Longsword: who would marry Sibylla?

During the following summer William Longsword died, a major blow to the royal family. Sibylla was pregnant and in 1178 she gave birth to a son, Baldwin. Now, not only was the kingdom ruled by a terminally ill leper-king who would gradually become disabled, but his heir was an infant, and unlikely to survive into adulthood given the conditions of the age. The race was on, therefore, to find a suitable husband for Sibylla who could father the next king and stay alive long enough to protect the kingdom. The first choice was Duke Hugh of Burgundy, nephew to the queen of France, but he failed to turn up. When Raymond of Tripoli and Bohemond III of Antioch arrived in Jerusalem to push for Raymond's candidate, Balian of Ibelin, King Baldwin blocked them by choosing Guy of Lusignan, brother to Almaric, the royal constable, but an outsider to the Holy Land.

Faction politics: the 'hawks' and the 'doves'

The rejection of Raymond's candidate and the marriage of Guy and Sibylla in 1180 created a fault line that ran right through the kingdom to the fateful year of 1187. The divided parties have traditionally been called the 'hawks' (who favoured war) and the 'doves' (who favoured peace). The 'hawks' included Guy, an outsider; **Reynald of Chatillon**; King Baldwin's mother, Agnes; and the Master of the Templars, Gerard de Ridefort. The 'doves' included the peace-makers Raymond of Tripoli; the Ibelins; and William of Tyre, chancellor and historian. This division between hawks and doves is not always clear-cut: the so-called 'hawks' favoured peace treaties as much as the so-called 'doves' pushed for war at times. The real division was a family matter; on the one side was King Baldwin's mother's family and on the other side were his cousins on his father's side (Raymond and Bohemond III).

BIOGRAPHY

Reynald of Chatillon (c.1125–87)

A French nobleman who came to Outremer as an outsider. He married Constance, the widowed heiress of Antioch, in 1153. Reynald was an uncontrollable, murderous barbarian who evoked the hatred and enmity of the Byzantines, crusaders, clergy and Muslims and eventually brought down the kingdom in 1187. In 1156 he ravaged Byzantine Cyprus, killing the Byzantine governor. For this he was forced to pay homage to the Emperor Manuel, damaging the good relations between Outremer and Byzantium. In 1157 he destroyed the possibility of a successful crusader invasion of northern Syria during an illness of Nur ad-Din because he insisted on retaining full powers over any conquests rather than submitting to King Baldwin III. He tortured Aimery, the ageing Patriarch of Antioch, by tying him to the top of the citadel, smearing him in honey and releasing a hive of bees on to him. Between 1160 and 1175 he was held captive by the Muslims and emerged a fanatical enemy of Islam. When he acquired the lordship of Transjordan this gave him a crucial base in the south of the kingdom from where he launched brutal attacks on Muslim caravans (the raid in the Red Sea in 1183 was Reynald's plan). The last of these, in 1187, provoked the successful invasion of the crusader kingdom by Saladin. Reynald was captured at the Battle of Hattin and was personally executed by Saladin, who had sworn to kill him.

Figure 9.1   Reynald tortures the Patriarch of Antioch (from a thirteenth-century manuscript).

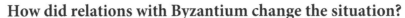

How did relations with Byzantium change the situation?

Relations with the Byzantine Empire had been much improved since the Second Crusade. King Baldwin III had married the Emperor Manuel's niece, Theodora, in 1158, and in the following year the combined armies of Byzantium, Jerusalem and Antioch marched on Aleppo, reinforcing the Byzantine overlordship of the Antioch rulers and forcing Nur ad-Din to allow an Orthodox patriarch in the city, although the crusaders failed to capture Aleppo. In 1167 King Amalric married Maria, another niece of Emperor Manuel, and in 1169 a joint Byzantine and crusader army attacked Damietta, in northern Egpyt, but without success. The close alliance between Byzantium and Jerusalem was illustrated by the journey of King Amalric to Constantinople in 1171. This was something no previous king of Jerusalem had ever done. It also shows the crusaders' desperate need of help, and it is possible that Amalric acknowledged the overlordship of the Emperor in order to gain the support he needed to deal with Nur ad-Din.

Amalric died in 1174 and in 1180 Emperor Manuel, his close ally, also died. The crusader kingdom thus lost its chief supporter. Manuel left a young son, Alexius, who was governed by his mother, Maria. She continued pro-crusader diplomacy, but after 1184 Saladin made a treaty with Byzantium, leaving the Holy Land without Byzantine support.

The regencies of Guy and Raymond

In 1180 a peace treaty was agreed with Saladin so that internal divisions within the kingdom could be healed. By 1183 Baldwin's leprosy was inflicting terrible agonies on the young man; he was blind and had lost the use of his hands and feet and was forced to appoint a regent, though he did not abdicate. The regent Baldwin chose was Guy, his brother-in-law. Guy was an outsider who had little experience of Outremer. Guy summoned the entire Christian forces from all over the kingdom and troops from Antioch and Tripoli, a total of some 17,000 men, to face a new threat from Saladin that summer. There was no battle and Saladin withdrew due to a lack of supplies. This appeared to be a success, but Guy's enemies persuaded Baldwin that there should have been a battle with Saladin to justify such a gathering of troops and destruction of crops, and Guy was removed as regent. Baldwin's young nephew, another Baldwin, was crowned co-king and by 1185 it was clear that Guy was well out of favour with Baldwin, who now wanted to annul Guy's marriage with Sibylla. He was close to death, and a strong leader was needed to act as regent, so once again Raymond of Tripoli was appointed, even though some barons distrusted him. In May 1185 Baldwin died, finished off by his leprosy at the age of 23. He was succeeded by his nephew, Baldwin V. Raymond, as regent, arranged a truce with Saladin, but in the summer of 1186 Baldwin V, aged nine, died.

The downfall of Raymond and Guy's coronation

The conditions of Raymond's regency stipulated that on Baldwin V's premature death, a council of western leaders, including the pope and the rulers of England, France and Germany should decide which of Baldwin IV's sisters, Sibylla or Isabella, should succeed. Raymond was in the north, gathering his supporters, but in Jerusalem support for Sibylla was strong, though her husband, Guy, was less popular. The nobles said that they would accept her as queen if she divorced Guy. Sibylla agreed, but reserved the right to choose her new husband. The divorce went ahead and the Patriarch of Jerusalem, Heraclius, crowned her queen, asking her to choose her regent and future husband. She chose – Guy! – placing the crown on his head so that he could be anointed by the Patriarch. This charade had clearly been planned by Sibylla, Guy and the Patriarch. It fooled the nobles and above all, Raymond, who had argued that Sibylla's sister Isabella should be queen and her husband,

Humphrey of Toron, therefore the new king. Humphrey, however, offered his loyalty to Guy: Raymond had been totally outmanoeuvred. Worse still, it was rumoured that Raymond had done a deal with Saladin to gain his support for the throne.

How did the crisis of 1187 occur?

The destruction of the crusader castle at Jacob's Ford demonstrated Saladin's might, but the annexation of Aleppo and Mosul in 1181–83 put a seal on his rise to power and successful uniting of the Muslim world. He was successfully encircling and increasingly threatening Outremer. The sharp decline in Baldwin IV's health was certainly to Saladin's advantage, but ultimately his greatest asset was the ability of the leaders of the crusader kingdom to bring about their own downfall.

Reynald's attack on the Muslim caravan (1187)

The truce of 1186 with Saladin was abruptly shattered by the rash and violent actions of Reynald of Chatillon, who attacked a Muslim caravan that was travelling from Cairo to Damascus, killing merchants, traders and women. This gave Saladin the opportunity to invade the kingdom, first besieging Kerak, Reynald's castle in the Transjordan, and then raiding through Galilee towards Acre. In response, the military orders raised a force of 500 men and took on 7000 Muslims at the Springs of Cresson on 1 May. The Christian force met with total defeat: only four knights got out alive. This senseless massacre depleted the overstretched forces of Outremer even further. In June, Saladin gathered his main armies from Egypt, Aleppo and Syria. Years of careful consolidation and diplomacy had brought him men, money and tremendous prestige. He had built up a reputation as the true defender of Islam and enemy of the Christians: his time had come at last.

The crusaders' dilemma: why did they risk a battle?

The Christians had a choice: to remain in the castles and walled towns and wait for Saladin's forces to run out of food whilst hoping that they themselves would get reinforcements from the West, or to march and confront Saladin in one great battle. The second option was extremely risky; the crusaders could not defend the towns and castles as well as field an effective army. If they lost the battle, they would lose the whole kingdom.

King Guy summoned the entire fighting force of Outremer, about 17,000 knights and men-at-arms, stripping the castle and town garrisons and using the treasure that had been sent by Henry II of England as his penance for the murder of Becket. Saladin's army numbered around 20,000 men; it was in his interest to force a decisive outcome and strike a massive blow for the cause of the jihad. He used the siege of Tiberias as bait, trapping Raymond of Tripoli's wife in the town on 2 July. However, Raymond, who had advised peace in 1183, counselled shadowing the enemy and waiting for them to go home, and Guy agreed to this.

Guy changes his mind: the fate of the kingdom is sealed

Guy, an outsider and king only in his wife's name, was haunted by his failure to deal with Saladin in 1183 when he had not gone into battle and had instead lost his position as regent. On the night of 2 July, two men convinced him that this time he would have to go to battle. One of them was, predictably, Reynald of Chatillon; the other was Gerard de Ridefort, master of the Templars. Both were uncompromising anti-Muslims, but they were also opponents of Raymond. Gerard may have remembered the fact that as a young knight he had been promised marriage to an important heiress in Tripoli, Lucia, who was Raymond's ward. Lucia had offered her weight in gold (63 kilograms) to gain her free choice in marriage and had chosen to marry a Pisan merchant instead of Gerard. Humiliated and filled with hatred of Raymond, Gerard joined the Templars. It was Guy and Gerard who had released Henry II's treasure, and now they had to justify that expenditure. Guy gave the order in the morning to march on Tiberias. Tiberias was 20 miles away on a road without water supplies, and Guy was playing straight into Saladin's hands.

What happened at the Battle of Hattin?

On 3 July 1187, the Muslim army continually attacked the crusader army, their archers wheeling back and forth. The Christians suffered dreadfully in the midsummer heat and were severely depleted. The Muslims' supplies were easily transported from Lake Tiberias.

Sources

B **Baha ad-Din, Saladin's biographer, writing in the early thirteenth century, describes the plight of the Christian army:**

They [the crusaders] were closely beset as in a noose, while still marching on as though being driven to a death that they could see before them, convinced of their doom and destruction and themselves aware that the following day they would be visiting their graves.

C **A local Frank, named Ernoul, writing soon after 1197, describes the battle scene:**

When the fires were lit and the smoke was great, the Saracens surrounded the host and shot their darts through the smoke and so wounded and killed men and horses. When the king saw the disadvantageous position the host was in, he called the master of the Temple and Prince Reynald and told them to give him their advice. They counselled him that he must fight the Saracens. When the king was aware that Saladin was coming against him he ordered the count of Tripoli to charge. The count and his division charged at a large squadron of Saracens. The Saracens parted and made a way through and let them pass; then, when they were in the middle of them, they surrounded them. After this division had been defeated

the anger of God was so great against the Christian host because of their sins that Saladin vanquished them quickly; between the hours of tierce and nones [i.e. between 9 a.m. and 3 p.m.] he had won almost all the field. He captured the King, the Master of the Temple, Prince Reynald, Marquis Boniface, Aimery the constable, Humphrey of Toron, Hugh of Gibelet, Plivain, lord of Botron, and so many other barons and knights that it would take too long to give the names of all of them; the Holy Cross also was lost.

D **The defeat at Hattin. Imad ad-Din, writing in the 1190s, graphically describes the nature of medieval warfare:**

The plain was covered with prisoners and corpses, disclosed by the dust as it settled and victory became clear. The dead were scattered over the mountains and valleys, lying immobile on their sides. I passed by them and saw the limbs of the fallen cast naked on the field of battle, scattered in pieces over the site of the encounter, lacerated and disjointed, with heads cracked open, throats split, spines broken, necks shattered, feet in pieces, noses mutilated, extremities torn off, members dismembered, parts shredded, eyes gouged out ... the chests smashed, bodies cut in half, arms pulverised, lips shrivelled, foreheads pierced ...

ACTIVITY
Using Sources B and C, assess how far the Battle of Hattin was won by the mistakes of the crusaders rather than the skilful tactics of Saladin.

The next day the crusaders planned to break out from the Muslim encirclement, but when the Muslims set the grass alight, the discomfort of the previous day and dehydration were now extreme. The infantry scattered whilst Raymond charged the enemy, breaking through and escaping (some thought that Saladin allowed him to get away). The remaining crusaders retreated to the twin peaks known as the Horns of Hattin, where Guy pitched his tent and charged down at Saladin himself, in the hope of killing the Muslim leader and thus ending the battle. This gamble failed: the Muslims attacked and captured Guy, Reynald and many nobles, Templars and Hospitallers and the True Cross (a prized relic that the Christians carried into battle).

Wise and magnanimous though Saladin undoubtedly was, the Templar and Hospitaller knights captured at Hattin could expect no mercy, and it was clear that Saladin would give them none. He personally dispatched the hated Reynard before giving the order to execute the knights of the military orders. By contrast, King Guy was given a glass of iced sherbet and escorted into honourable captivity.

Source

(E) **Imad ad-Din, writing in the 1190s, describes the execution of the Templar and Hospitaller prisoners after Hattin:**

Saladin, his face joyful, was sitting on his dais; the unbelievers showed black despair, the troops were drawn up in their ranks, the emirs stood in double file. There were some who slashed and cut cleanly, and were thanked for it ... I saw how [they] killed unbelief to give life to Islam, and drove decisions through to their conclusion to satisfy the community of the faithful and cut down the enemies in the defence of friends!

Saladin's victory was absolute. As a fellow king, Guy was treated with respect, but members of the military orders were all executed – something everyone expected – and the remaining nobles were sold into slavery. There was no mercy for Reynald, the most psychotic and murderous crusader: Saladin used a scimitar to sever his arm at the shoulder before his bodyguards hacked off his head.

Figure 9.2   The Horns of Hattin today.

The fall of Jerusalem

The crusader kingdom was now utterly exposed. Saladin's army marched through Tiberias, Nazareth, Acre, Caesarea and Jaffa, taking all the coastal towns except Tyre, which held out under the leadership of Conrad of Montferrat, brother of William Longsword. Saladin did not waste time in sieges; he simply moved on and isolated any towns that did not surrender immediately.

Jerusalem held out, but with only two knights and the civilian population its fall was only a matter of time. Heraclius agreed the city's surrender. and many Christians were ransomed if they could afford to pay, or enslaved if not. There was no mass slaughter as there had been when the crusaders captured the city in 1099, but the choices for the inhabitants were grim. Those who could not afford to pay the ransom became slaves (including children) and mass rape of the women was not prevented. No Latin (western Christian) was allowed to remain, though some eastern Christians could. Christian churches were converted into mosques or stables, and convents or teaching colleges were stripped of their valuables. Saladin installed a *minbar* (pulpit) in the Temple Church which had been the al-Aqsa mosque before 1099, the site of Muhammad's ascension to heaven. The church of the Holy Sepulchre was spared (again, in contrast to the destruction and slaughter of 1099) and Christian pilgrims were allowed to visit on payment of a fee.

> ### Source
>
> (F) **Imad ad-Din, writing in the 1190s, describes the conquering Muslims' treatment of Jerusalem and its inhabitants:**
>
> *... the churches and the altars became stables for the horses and cattle and places of debauchery, drinking and singing. Added to which was the shame and derision of the monks, of noblewomen, of pure nuns who were delivered into impurity with all sorts of people, of boys and girls who became Turkish slaves and were dispersed to the four corners of earth.*

Saladin was careful to ensure that he dealt with the Christians in Jerusalem harshly, so as to confirm his position as leader of the jihad. Jerusalem had become more significant as a holy city of Islam over the decades since 1099, and Saladin used its capture to demonstrate his power to the Arab world.

> ### ACTIVITY
>
> 1   Use Sources D–F to assess how the Muslim writers regarded the defeated crusaders.
>
> 2   To what extent did Saladin exploit the idea of the jihad to further his own ends?

More crusader castles surrendered in 1188, 1189 and 1190 but those in northern Syria, including the great Hospitaller fortress of Krak des Chevaliers, held out. And, most significantly for the beleaguered Christians, the port of Tyre remained in crusader hands, providing a foothold for the armies of the Third Crusade.

Source

(G) From Jean Richard, *The Crusades c1071–c1291*:

The westerners had frequent experience of the opposition between their own intentions – to earn their remission by fighting in God's service – and those of the Franks of the East, who did not hesitate to make truces with the Muslims and refused to break them so as to give their allies an opportunity to fight, thereby rendering vain the sacrifices they had made.

(H) From T. Jones & A. Ereira, *Crusades*

It was unfortunate for the kingdom that the twenty-one-year-old King Baldwin IV was a leper. In recent years his terrible disease had become so bad that he had been persuaded to hand over the reins of the kingdom to his sister Sibylla's husband, Guy de Lusignan – a man 'unequal to the burden both in force and in wisdom' in the rather jaundiced view of William of Tyre.

ACTIVITY

From your reading of the Conclusion and Sources G and H above, rank the causes of the collapse of the kingdom in order, with the most important at the top.

Conclusion

The downfall of Outremer, the crusader kingdom established after 1100, was total. It was never recovered even partly, despite many more crusades from the West. A Christian army was not to enter Jerusalem again for over 700 years.

The collapse of the kingdom was by no means inevitable, even in 1186, after years of a diseased and feeble king embroiled in disputes with leading nobles over his regency and succession. Saladin was defeated by crusader armies in 1177 and 1182; Reynald's daring raid down the Red Sea in 1183 had damaged Saladin's prestige as defender of the Islamic faith. The campaign of 1183 had ended inconclusively.

Long-term and short-term factors did however contribute to the final collapse:

Long-term:

■ Nur ad-Din's efforts in building the jihad and uniting Egpyt with Syria (1146–74) paid off under Saladin, but this still took ten years for him to achieve (1174–84).

■ The constant appeals to the West failed to gather enough support and outside help was diminished further by the breakdown of relations with Byzantium.

Short-term:

■ The marriage of Guy and Sibylla triggered faction and dissent among the nobles which was never resolved, leaving the leadership of the kingdom in 1187 simmering with distrust and resentment.

■ Reynald of Chatillon was out of control; a strong king, sure of his authority, would have dealt with him.

■ The decision to march out to Tiberias was disastrous; Guy made the choice based on advice from the 'hawks' and to slay his own demons because of his insecure position as king.

The reign of Baldwin IV, the leper-king, and his short-lived young nephew, Baldwin V, were not necessarily the cause of the downfall in 1187, although Baldwin IV's decision to allow Guy to marry his sister was certainly the wrong choice. The continual shortage of men was not in the end an issue, because Saladin's advantage of 5000 troops was not overwhelming. Guy could have chosen to shadow Saladin as he did in 1183, waited for him to retire and executed Reynald. Perhaps the right moment might never have come again for Saladin, who would not have had the excuse he had in 1187 or the support from the Islamic world.

However, the fateful decision was made and Jerusalem was lost. It would now take the might of the western world, after so many years of prevarication, to attempt to regain the kingdom of Jerusalem in the Third Crusade.

Review questions

1   To what extent was the failure of the West to send aid a result of political and not religious motivation?

2   To what extent did the crusaders' mistakes rather than Saladin's tactics ensure Saladin's victory at Hattin?

3   How far do you agree that the fall of Jerusalem was due more to long-term than short-term factors?

> **Key Questions:**
>
> In this chapter you will learn:
>
> - How the West responded to the fall of Jerusalem
> - Why the Third Crusade faced such difficulties
> - How political rivalries weakened the crusade
> - Why Richard failed to recapture Jerusalem
>
> You will also develop the following skills:
>
> - Assessing the language and tone of documents
> - Comparing sources and their limitations
> - Analysing the impact of individuals
> - Making a judgement on the failure to recapture Jerusalem

Introduction

In the period 1190–93 the greatest-ever crusade in Europe was launched against the Muslim East, with the combined might of France, Germany and, for the first time, Britain. In addition many other nationalities joined, including Austrians, Italians, and Flemish. The planning and the finances were meticulously organised over several years and the greatest names in western Europe led the expedition. Crusading had transformed from the armed pilgrimage of 1095 into a highly sophisticated military mission. The participants were now trained soldiers on regular pay, rather than the spontaneous mass movement that characterised the First Crusade.

Vast reserves were mobilised, and the crusaders had the single, clear objective of recapturing Jerusalem (unlike the failed Second Crusade). Yet all the hopes and strategies of the crusaders faded into failure for the following reasons:

- Saladin's resources from Egypt, Syria and Yemen proved too great.
- The squabbling and political differences between the western leaders destroyed their very strength.
- The German contingent was dealt a fatal blow at the start when their emperor, the feared Frederick Barbarossa, suffered a heart attack and died while crossing a river in Turkey on the journey to the Holy Land.
- The final ignominy was the two-year imprisonment of King Richard I of England, the most successful military man of his age, by Count Leopold of Austria.

However, the crusade was not a total failure. Richard defeated Saladin in battle, retained several coastal ports and castles and forced Saladin to a peace treaty. This proved to the Muslim world that the West was still a force to be reckoned with and left a foot in the door for future crusades. Richard himself promised to return and exploit his gains (the death of Saladin in 1193 certainly would have made this a possibility), but increasing political divisions in western Europe made this unfeasible for Richard.

Chapter timeline

July 1187	Battle of Hattin.
September 1187	Fall of Jerusalem; Pope Gregory VIII launches the Third Crusade.
1189	Henry II of England dies, succeeded by his son, Richard I.
June 1190	German Emperor Frederick Barbarossa dies leading the German contingent across Asia Minor, leaving German troops in disarray.
September 1190	Richard and King Philip of France leave for the Holy Land.
May 1191	Richard captures Cyprus, a useful crusader base for the future.
June 1191	Richard arrives at Acre and captures the port in July, executing 3000 Muslim prisoners; Philip leaves the Holy Land.
September 1191	Richard defeats Saladin at the Battle of Arsuf; first march on Jerusalem begins.
January 1192	March on Jerusalem fails.
April 1192	Conrad of Montferrat murdered.
May 1192	Second march on Jerusalem fails.
August 1192	Richard captures Jaffa.
September 1192	Three-year truce signed.
October 1192	Richard leaves the Holy Land.

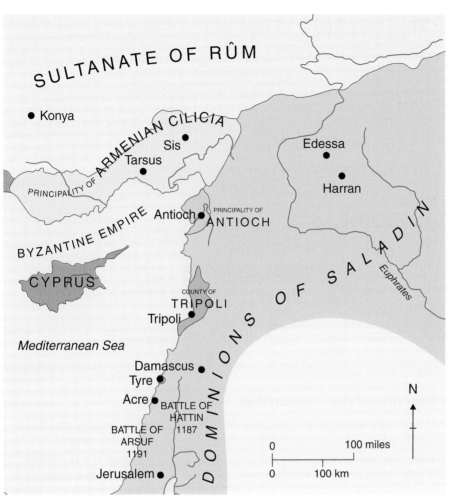

Figure 10.1   The Near East in 1190.

KEY ISSUES

- What was the initial reaction of the West?
- How did Richard of England prepare for the crusade?
- How significant was the death of Frederick Barbarossa?
- How far did the political disputes between Guy and Conrad of Montferrat weaken the crusade?
- Why did it take so long for the western armies to arrive?
- Why was Richard unable to recapture Jerusalem?
- How far was the Third Crusade a failure?

What was the initial reaction of the West?

In October 1187 Pope Gregory VIII issued a crusader bull, *Audita tremendi*. It repeated Urban II's message of 1095 about the penitential war, and promised indulgences and protection for crusaders' land and families, as Bernard of Clairvaux had done for the

Second Crusade (1145–48). Preachers followed up the official message with their own lurid propaganda and refugees arrived from the Holy Land with tales of Muslim atrocities. (They probably omitted the fact that Saladin had not committed wholesale slaughter in the Holy City after the Battle of Hattin as the crusaders had done in 1099.) The Archbishop of Canterbury toured Wales in 1188, calling for a crusade. Jews in England were victims of massacres in Stamford and King's Lynn, and in York hundreds of Jews committed suicide to avoid slaughter. The Jews were blamed for being the descendants of the killers of Christ; they were also envied for having ready cash, which the crusaders badly needed.

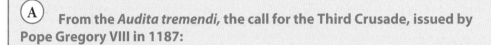

Source

(A) **From the *Audita tremendi*, the call for the Third Crusade, issued by Pope Gregory VIII in 1187:**

But to those who with contrite hearts and humbled spirits undertake the journey and die in penitence for their sins and right faith we promise full indulgence of their faults and eternal life; whether surviving or dying they shall know that, through the mercy of almighty God and the authority of the apostles Peter and Paul, and our authority, they will have the relaxation of the reparation imposed for all their sins, of which they have made proper confession …

Why was the crusade slow in starting?

The response to the appeal was the greatest since 1095; kings Henry of England and Philip of France vowed to take the cross, and so did the Emperor Frederick Barbarossa of Germany. But despite this response and clear leadership from the papacy, it was another two and a half years before the first effective crusader armies set out to recapture the Holy Land.

The perennial differences between England and France dominated even the fall of Jerusalem. The new king of France, Philip (son of the second crusader Louis VII, whose first wife Eleanor had remarried Henry II of England) was determined to hound Henry II to his death, aided by Henry's treacherous sons Richard and John. Henry died alone at Chinon in July 1189, deserted by his family, but the moment Richard became king, the considerable wealth of the **Angevin Empire** could now be channelled into the crusade.

Angevin Empire

The so-called Angevin Empire came about through marriage, inheritance and conquest in the 1150s. Henry II was the grandson of King Henry I of England and the son of Count Geoffrey of Anjou. His father had conquered Normandy from King Stephen of England and in 1154 Henry inherited England, Normandy and Anjou. Henry's marriage to Eleanor, duchess of Aquitaine, brought him most of south-western France, making him ruler of lands that stretched from Hadrian's Wall to the Pyrenees. Henry's son Richard was a brilliant soldier who held the empire together, but his youngest son John succeeded Richard in 1199 and lost it all to France in 1204.

How did Richard of England prepare for the crusade?

Richard I of England was at the height of his powers when he succeeded his father in 1189. In his early thirties, he had spent his adult life perfecting the art of war and understood well the necessities of logistical campaigns; he knew that this crusade would be the military expedition of his life.

Richard was not only king of England (where he spent only ten months of his ten-year reign) but also duke of Normandy, Aquitaine and Anjou and count of Touraine. This gave him access to vast resources, far more than were available to King Philip of France. Richard's army would prove to be the best-resourced and best-led crusading army of all and, for the first time, would include British troops on a crusade. The death of Henry II had for the time being put an end to the Anglo-French rivalry and Richard's preparations, which had been two years in the making, were meticulous:

- The Jews of England were taxed heavily.
- All those of military age not taking the Cross were fined (except those with essential administrative roles).
- A fleet of 100 ships was hired and purchased to avoid travelling across Europe; this eliminated peasants and useless non-combatants who would get in the way of the professional troops, as had happened in the first two crusades.
- 60,000 horseshoes were purchased, mainly from the Forest of Dean, Gloucestershire, and 14,000 cured pig carcasses were brought from Lincolnshire, Essex and Hampshire in 1190.

In April 1191, Richard gathered his army of 17,000 troops in Sicily. The army consisted of the military households of the nobles, plus Welsh archers and mercenaries. Philip had fewer resources than Richard, but negotiated with the Genoese to transport 650 knights, 1300 **squires** and 1300 horses with provisions for eight months.

> **Source**
>
> **(B)** Roger of Howden, writing in the 1190s, describes the extent of Richard I's fund-raising for the Third Crusade:
>
> *He [Richard] put up for sale all he had, offices, lordships, earldoms, sheriffdoms, castles, towns, lands, everything.*

How significant was the death of Frederick Barbarossa?

The greatest military leader in Christendom was not actually Richard of England but the Holy Roman Emperor, the hugely respected and experienced Frederick Barbarossa. Frederick had been emperor for 36 years. He had taken part in the Second Crusade and commanded 20,000 men, including 3000 knights, the largest army the West could send.

The German contingent crossed by land into Asia Minor where they defeated the Turks in a decisive battle near Iconium (modern Konya) in May 1190. But while crossing a river near Silifke in June, the Emperor had a heart attack and drowned. His vast army broke up, and many of the soldiers returned home, though his son continued with a portion of the army to relieve the siege of Acre.

squires

Young men, sometimes teenagers from noble families, who cleaned the knights' weapons and tended their war-horses. Each knight had with him several squires, who would ride into battle close behind their lord. In time, the squires would expect to be knighted and find a position in a great nobleman's household, or be granted land of their own to live off.

ACTIVITY

How far did the preparations for the Third Crusade reflect the difficulties facing the crusaders?

The death of Barbarossa had a significant impact on the crusade for the following reasons:

- He had the greatest army, which would have been a real threat to Saladin and combined with Richard's force may well have altered the course of the crusade.
- Frederick was the most experienced and prestigious Christian warrior, and could have dealt with the political squabbling that divided the crusade later on.
- Frederick also managed to impose his authority on the hostile Byzantine Empire.

How far did the political disputes between Guy and Conrad of Montferrat weaken the crusade?

In what was left of Outremer, a small army was fighting a last-ditch stand against the might of the victorious Muslim army. Soon after the disastrous Battle of Hattin in 1187, **Conrad of Montferrat** landed at Tyre and forced Saladin's troops back, providing a foothold for the crusading army in the Holy Land.

BIOGRAPHY
Conrad of Montferrat

Conrad was the brother of the deceased William Longsword who had married Sibylla in 1176 (see page 108). He had connections with both the French and German ruling dynasties. After King Guy was captured at the Battle of Hattin, Conrad assumed leadership of the kingdom. His heroic deeds were celebrated throughout Europe, spurring on the West to rouse themselves against Islam. Conrad married Sibylla's sister Isabella to strengthen his claim, but was murdered in 1192.

Who would be king of Jerusalem?

One of the overriding issues of the Third Crusade was the question of who would be the king of Jerusalem (assuming that the Holy City would be recaptured, of course). In June 1188 Saladin released Guy, who went immediately to Tyre to assert his authority over Conrad. Conrad refused to hand over the town. Guy marched to Acre, which was now in Muslim hands, and laid siege to it, digging in and holding out. But when Sibylla and her daughters died during the siege in the winter of 1190, Guy was left without his principal claim to the throne, which was only through his marriage to Sibylla. Now the claim rested with Sibylla's sister, Isabella, who was married to Humphrey of Toron.

Conrad's marriage to Isabella

There followed another dramatic turn of events when Conrad abducted Isabella. Her marriage to Humphrey was annulled by a Pisan churchman, and then in December 1190 Isabella married Conrad, even though Conrad's wife was probably still alive.

Richard and Philip's allegiances

The big question then, was who Richard and Philip would support when they finally arrived. The decisions were already made for them because, in the tradition of medieval Europe, family connections dictated political decisions. Guy was from the town of Poitiers, which was within Richard's jurisdiction as duke of Aquitaine, so Guy gained Richard's

ACTIVITY
Assess the importance of family connections in the politics of the kingdom of Jerusalem.

support. Conrad was related to Philip and therefore got his backing. The temporary peace between the kings of England and France was already strained, and the death of Barbarossa removed a crucial referee in what turned out to be a very ugly and divisive dispute before the city of Jerusalem was even recaptured – which, as things turned out, it never was.

Why did it take so long for the western armies to arrive?

While the sieges of Tyre and Acre dragged on through the period 1190–91, Philip and Richard and their armies took a year to get across the Mediterranean. They left the shores of southern France in July 1190, but Richard halted at Sicily from September 1190 to April 1191. This was because the ruler of Sicily, Tancred, owed Richard a large sum of money, and Richard needed this to help finance the crusade. In addition, Richard had with him the sword **Excalibur** and suggested to Tancred that he give him four ships in return for the sword, thereby gaining even more supplies for the journey. The crusader army then remained in port for the winter and sailed in April. However, when some of the fleet was blown ashore in Cyprus in a storm and Richard's men were mistreated by the Byzantine Emperor Isaac Comnenus, who was allied to Saladin, Richard stormed the island. He eventually captured it and sold part of it to the Templars for 100,000 besants. This not only demonstrated the wealth of the Templars – and Richard's canny financial gain – but shows that Richard's thinking was very long-term. Cyprus provided an ideal base for crusading armies to use when supplying and reinforcing expeditions to the Holy Land. It was while Richard was at Cyprus that Guy turned up, seeking Richard's support to help him hold on to the crown of Jerusalem.

Excalibur

The sword that had belonged to the legendary King Arthur, giving him magical powers in battle. Arthur was a Romano-British chieftain who fought the Saxon invaders in the mid-fifth century. He became known as a heroic chivalric king in England during the twelfth century, and stories about him and his Knights of the Round Table were popular.

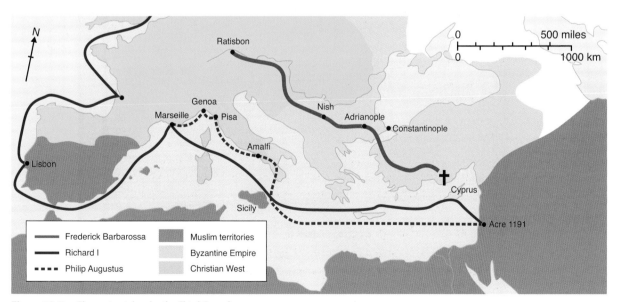

Figure 10.2 The routes taken by the Third Crusade.

Why was Richard unable to recapture Jerusalem?

The main objective of the Third Crusade was the recapture of Jerusalem and the re-establishment of the crusader kingdom. The death of Barbarossa in 1190 would have lasting repercussions on the success of the crusade, and the contest between Guy and Conrad – mirrored by the contesting support of Richard and Philip – would further weaken the crusade. The first task would be to capture Acre and then to draw Saladin into battle, hoping for a decisive defeat, but it was not necessarily the taking of Jerusalem that would be the greatest problem – it was holding it. Richard was well aware of this, and it was this that ultimately defeated him.

The siege of Acre

Richard arrived at Acre in June 1191, two years after Guy had begun the assault. Conditions had been dreadful – disease and famine had killed thousands, including Sibylla and her daughters. The besieging crusaders and the Muslims defending the town and encircling the besiegers could not make any breakthrough. The arrival of Philip of France – who tended to win campaigns more by cunning and deceit than by brute military skill – made little difference. It was Richard's expertise that finished the job; the Muslims had dreaded his arrival and Saladin had done all he could to wipe out the attackers before he arrived. Richard's money, siege machines and leadership forced the surrender of the city in July, after a month of bombardment, **mining** and repeated assaults. The defenders paid heavy ransoms for their lives and returned 1500 Frankish prisoners and the True Cross captured at Hattin. It was a great triumph for the crusaders.

mining

A technique for bringing down sections of a castle or town wall. The besiegers would dig away the earth at the foot of the wall until they could tunnel underneath. They would put in wooden props to support their tunnel, then withdraw and set light to the props. The wall above would usually collapse at this point. Mining could be dangerous work for the diggers: their tunnel might collapse, and they were a sitting target for the defenders on the top of the wall.

Figure 10.3   The Siege of Acre.

The departure of Duke Leopold and King Philip

The campaign could not have got off to a better start for Richard, but from there on, things went downhill. Richard's men pulled down the banner of Count Leopold of Austria, claiming that even though Leopold had been at the siege longer than Richard, his status did not entitle him to fly his colours alongside the King of England. Leopold then left Outremer in a rage, taking his troops with him. (Eighteen months later he imprisoned Richard after the king was captured returning through Austria.) Then, in August 1191, Philip left the crusade. He complained of ill-health and said he had a dispute to settle in Flanders, but his absence was a severe blow to the crusade and his devious and scheming behaviour in Europe did little to help Richard. Before Philip departed, it was agreed that Guy would remain as king for his lifetime, to be succeeded by Conrad; they would share the royal income equally. Conrad was not happy with this and schemed behind Richard's back, negotiating independently with Saladin.

ACTIVITY

To what extent did the political rivalries of the leaders weaken the crusade?

The massacre of the prisoners

When Saladin failed to make the first ransom payment for the prisoners taken at Acre, Richard marched them out and slaughtered all 3000 of them. It took three days. Observers at the time were shocked by this brutality and criticised Richard. Richard had to push on to Jaffa and feeding and guarding the prisoners was a considerable burden to the crusaders, so it may have been that Saladin was deliberately delaying payment in order to keep Richard pinned down. However, the barbarity of the West was in stark contrast to the mercy shown to the inhabitants of Jerusalem when Saladin took the city in 1187.

The battle of Arsuf

In the heat of August, the crusader army marched south, supplied by their fleet which shadowed them along the coast. Saladin's army was continually attacking them, with his archers wheeling about and tempting the Christians to break ranks. The line held firm, with the Templars in the vanguard (front), Hospitallers in the rear, Richard's army and the troops of Jerusalem in the centre. Then, on 7 September, Saladin chose to fight an open battle and ordered a general assault on the crusaders. This time, the Hospitallers broke ranks and counter-attacked, and Richard was forced to order a general charge that swept the Muslims from the battlefield, with Richard personally leading the attack.

Why was Egypt important?

Richard arrived in Jaffa and refortified the town. As a military strategist of the highest ability, he fully realised that Egypt was the key to Saladin's wealth and resources. It was clear, therefore, that in order to keep Jerusalem after it was recaptured, Egypt would need to be conquered first. Richard was correct in this, and future crusades in the thirteenth century all focused their efforts on Egypt. Richard wrote to the **Genoese**, asking for a fleet to support a campaign in the summer of 1192, and offering many trading concessions in return. But the crusader army of 1191 was not interested in Egypt; Jerusalem was the draw. Negotiations with Saladin over custody of the Holy City came to nothing and Richard agreed to march on Jerusalem before campaigning in Egypt.

Genoese

Genoa was a city-state in northern Italy. It grew wealthy on maritime trade and had a powerful navy.

The first attempt to capture Jerusalem

The march began in late October, and by January the army was 15 miles away from Jerusalem. This was slow progress (Jaffa was only 50 miles from Jerusalem) but Richard was rightly being cautious, ensuring that his supply lines were protected and that the castles were refortified on the way. As the army got nearer to Jerusalem, the crusaders realised that once recaptured, the Holy City would be impossible to defend. They decided to turn back. The military orders and the nobles of Outremer argued that the coast needed consolidating, but those who had come from the West, having taken their vows to go to Jerusalem, were devastated.

ACTIVITY

Why does Source C say that the army might have been 'less troubled by anxiety' if they had known about the state of the Muslims in Jerusalem?

Source

C   **An anonymous account from the thirteenth century tells how the Third Crusade turned back from Jerusalem:**

However, when the army was actually informed about the decision to retreat, the common people pined away with indescribable grief. All sighed and groaned because their heartfelt hope of visiting the Lord's Sepulchre had suddenly been ended.

Yet if these people had been more fully informed about the poor state of those Muslims who were in Jerusalem, they would have been less troubled by anxiety and taken some comfort from their enemies' adversities. The Turks who had shut themselves in Jerusalem were indeed in the direst straits … without doubt, the long-desired city of Jerusalem could have been easily captured. Yet it could not have been held by our people for long, because when the pilgrimage was completed the people would have gone home and there would not have been anyone left who could defend it.

The murder of Conrad

Richard refortified Ascalon, but bad news had come from Europe: King Philip of France was threatening Normandy and Richard's younger brother John was stirring up rebellion in England – so much for papal protection for absentee crusaders. Guy's support had drained away and Richard had finally acknowledged Conrad as the new king of the yet-to-be-captured Jerusalem, while Guy was given Cyprus. But on 28 April 1192, Conrad was murdered by two Assassins (see pages 99 and 100) in the streets of Tyre. It is unknown who ordered the murder – it may have been Saladin or the Assassins themselves who had a reason to kill him – but Richard was suspected so strongly that when he left the Holy Land he had to travel back through Europe in disguise to avoid recriminations.

This reopened the succession issue again – a third husband was found for Isabella: Count Henry of Champagne. Henry was a nephew of both Richard and Philip and was well known in the Holy Land. (Isabella went on to have a fourth husband, Aimery of Lusignan, after Henry was knocked out of a window by his dwarfish entertainer in 1197.)

The second attempt on Jerusalem

Now that the succession matter was settled, Richard could focus on the campaign. He tried in vain to persuade the army to invade Egypt, but the French contingent refused. Again the crusader army came within sight of Jerusalem, but capturing it was not possible because of the logistics of holding it. The army withdrew to the coast again.

The Battle of Jaffa

At this point, making his first move in months, Saladin stormed the port of Jaffa and took the town, leaving just the citadel defended by a small crusader force. Richard responded with characteristic brilliance: sailing from Acre, he waded ashore leading a tiny assault force, and scattered the Muslim troops, who were overawed and overwhelmed by his courage and nerve.

Saladin attacked Ascalon but was also forced back by Richard's army, the King again in the thick of the action.

Sources

D **The thirteenth-century *Itinerarium* (Chronicle of the Third Crusade) describes Richard's counter-attack at Jaffa:**

With no armour on his legs he threw himself into the sea first … and forced his way onto dry land. The outstanding king shot [the Turks] down indiscriminately with a crossbow he was carrying in his hand, and his elite companions pursued the Turks as they fled across the beach, cutting them down.

E **The *Itinerarium* describes how Richard fought at Ascalon:**

On that day his sword shone like lightning and many of the Turks felt its edge. Some were cloven in two from their helmet to their teeth; others lost their heads, arms and other limbs, lopped off at a single blow.

Stalemate

Stuff of legends though Richard's deeds undoubtedly were, they did not regain Jerusalem or comprehensively defeat Saladin. A three-year truce was signed in September 1192, whereby it was agreed that the Christians would keep the coastline from Jaffa to Tyre (but would hand over Ascalon) and Christian pilgrims would be allowed to visit Jerusalem freely, though the city remained in Muslim hands. Richard did not visit Jerusalem; he left Outremer, vowing to return once he had sorted out the political problems back in Europe. He never did return to the Holy Land: he was killed by a crossbow-bolt in 1199. The greatest irony was that had Richard remained a little longer, he might have capitalised on the death of Saladin in March 1193, which utterly divided the Muslim world.

Saladin and Richard

Although the fall of Jerusalem was cataclysmic for the crusader kingdom and galvanised the West into belated action, contemporaries were fully aware that the conflict between the greatest Muslim leader, Saladin, and the most heroic Christian leader, Richard I, would be one for the poets and chroniclers to celebrate. The two leaders were seen as somehow above the welter of killing that took place at Hattin and Acre, but they never met. Both sides respected the two leaders greatly, even though they were engaged in deadly combat.

ACTIVITY

To what extent was a decisive victory by either Richard or Saladin always going to be an impossibiliity?

The King of England was a very powerful man among the Franks, a man of great courage and spirit. He had fought great battles, and showed a burning passion for war. His kingdom and standing were inferior to those of the French king, but his wealth, reputation and valour were greater ... he possessed judgement, experience, audacity and astuteness. To gain his ends sometimes he used soft words, at other times, violent deeds. God alone was able to save us from his malice. Never have we had to face a bolder or more subtle opponent.

Although Richard and Saladin did not meet, there were secret negotiations to arrange the possible marriage of Richard's sister Joan to Saladin's brother, but this never happened. Richard left the Holy Land vowing to return, and when Saladin died in 1193 much of the Muslim unity he had built up under the umbrella of the jihad began to crumble, but the West was in no position to exploit this.

Figure 10.4 A late medieval manuscript depicting Richard I and Saladin in combat, although it is unlikely they ever faced one another in battle.

ACTIVITY

Why might writers in the West and the East romanticise the conflict between Richard and Saladin?

Richard's imprisonment (December 1192–February 1194)

Richard travelled home in disguise but was recognised in Austria and imprisoned by Count Leopold, whose banner had been torn down after the capture of Acre. Leopold handed Richard over to the German Emperor Henry VI, who kept him prisoner until February 1194. This was a final stain on the crusading ideal and an ignominious end to the greatest of all the crusades. Richard was only released after payment of a vast ransom (paid for by English taxpayers, of course) and by handing over Cyprus. This gave the Germans what they wanted for their own crusade. This included 16,000 troops, and took Beirut in 1197, but it petered out when Emperor Henry died in September that year.

How far was the Third Crusade a failure?

Since it had failed to capture Jerusalem, the Third Crusade as a whole was a failure. The kingdom of Jerusalem, the provinces of Tripoli, Antioch and Edessa were now all lost. Most of the castles and fortified towns were now in Muslim hands.

However, several factors marked out the Third Crusade as a success:

- The Christians had secured the coastline from Jaffa to Tyre (but not Ascalon).
- Christian pilgrims were permitted to enter Jerusalem.
- Richard's defeats of Saladin at the battles of Acre, Arsuf and Jaffa had damaged Saladin's reputation.
- Richard's actions gained him great prestige in the Muslim world and, as it was believed that he would return, the territorial successes of the Third Crusade provided him with a platform from which to attack Islam.

Source

(G) **An Arab view of Richard I, by Baha ad-Din, writing in the thirteenth century:**

… he possessed judgement, experience, audacity and astuteness. To gain his ends sometimes he used soft words, at other times, violent deeds. God alone was able to save us from his malice. Never have we had to face a bolder or more subtle opponent.

Review questions

1. How far did the preparations for the Third Crusade reflect the difficulties facing the crusaders?
2. To what extent did the political rivalries of the leaders weaken the crusade?
3. Why did the Third Crusade fail to recapture Jerusalem?
4. How far was Saladin's authority diminished by the Third Crusade?
5. 'The Third Crusade failed mainly because of internal political divisions within the crusader army.' How far do you agree with this statement?

ExamCafé
Relax, refresh, result!

Relax and prepare

GETTING ORGANISED

Tom

I did well at GCSE without really pushing myself or doing much revision, so I guess I was a little overconfident about how I'd do at AS-level. I didn't think it would be so different and I was totally unprepared for how much I was expected to do by myself. I skipped some of the research homeworks we were set, wrote stuff at the last minute and managed to get by in lessons, but when I came to start revising I couldn't avoid the mess that my notes were in. There were gaps and half-finished bits and pieces all over the place. My advice would be to remember this: it isn't your teacher who's taking the exam – it's YOU! Unless you're prepared to make the extra effort, you aren't going to do brilliantly.

Rhiannon

The best piece of advice I'd give myself looking back at the start of the year? Easy – get a folder and get organised! The notes come really thick and fast and you need to collect them together properly. Just stuffing them in your bag or starting a new page of your refill pad every lesson won't do. They end up looking like scrap and they're useless for revision. I also wish I'd checked my notes over more outside of lessons and maybe rewritten some of them to make them clearer while the topic was still fresh in my mind.

READING SOURCES

Dave

I found it hard to concentrate on what a source was saying. My mind would wander off and I'd end up reading and re-reading the same bit without getting anywhere. So I found ways to keep my mind focused and my eyes on the text. I use a ruler and put it under the first line of the source then move it down to the next line and so on. That way, I only look at one part at a time. I also stop after every sentence and repeat back to myself what I have just read. I know some people use a highlighter as well, but I was highlighting everything! So I tend to write a running summary in the margin or on a piece of paper.

Ali

My teacher said that I was losing marks because I wasn't reading sources carefully enough. What she meant was that I was reading too quickly and missing useful information or ideas. I had to learn to slow down! What I do now is read the source through once at my usual speed without writing anything down. That gives me a general picture of what the source is about. Then I read it twice more – the first time I use a highlighter to pick out all the relevant points. Then – and here's the thing that really made a difference for me – I read it again but only the bits I haven't highlighted. That way, I can ask myself if I have missed anything out.

USING THE INTERNET

Mark

The internet is a great resource but watch out for dodgy websites. You have to ask yourself who is putting this information onto the web and why – so that you can avoid sites that are obviously biased. I used what looked like great websites, but I found out that some of them were written by amateurs who knew even less than me! Also, watch out for how long the information has been there – it could be stuff that's out of date.

Sunita

I printed loads of stuff off the internet to put in my file. Just one problem – I didn't actually read any of it! Using the internet was really just a way of avoiding making proper notes. Cutting and pasting stuff into a Word document made me feel I was motoring through the research, but I ended up binning most of it and starting again when I revised.

Jamie

I always used a textbook to make my notes from. The trouble was, I wasn't really learning how to do research. It took a bit of effort to go into the library and find out what was there – not just the books but magazine articles and online information – but it was worth it because that's what you'll have to do if you go to university. Things aren't always packaged for you.

GETTING DOWN TO STUDY

Sufia

I found it hard to settle down to study – there was always something more interesting that I could be doing. My teacher suggested using a ritual to get me started. Now what I do is make myself a cuppa when I want to start working. As the kettle is boiling I start thinking about what I need to do, so if it's an essay, I start thinking about what I'm going to write. By the time the drink's ready I've already started work and I can sit down and put pen to paper.

Jeff

I'm a morning person. I know that I can get up and start work straight away for a few hours; then my interest starts flagging. At night I'm too tired or distracted to work for very long. So I plan my study around how I am – essays and big tasks in the morning, finishing off and small tasks at night.

Asif

Break everything down into small tasks if you find it hard to get started. You aren't writing an essay, you're writing one paragraph. Get that done, congratulate yourself then write another paragraph! Keep taking short breaks – get up and walk about – and have a treat ready for when you've finished to motivate yourself to get through the work.

MAKING NOTES

Phil

I used to write notes that were basically just copies of the chapter I was reading! As soon as I started reading I just started writing and writing and writing – I might as well have just put a photocopy of the book in my file! I learned that the best way to make notes was not to have a pen in my hand – read everything first, think about what seems important to keep a record of, THEN write it down!

Catherine

I have some really colourful notes – I took a highlighter and marked all the important things. Unfortunately, nearly everything has ended up being highlighted! I'm going to use colour more sparingly from now on – maybe just for key words or quotes.

Jas

A good piece of advice is to write notes on one side of paper and leave the reverse blank. That way, when the pages are in your file there's always a blank sheet on the left-hand side that you can use to add extra stuff later.

STRUCTURING ANSWERS

Jane

Everyone sort of expects you to know this, but I was really stuck about how to put paragraphs in my answers. This is the advice I got – each paragraph is for a new idea in your answer (like a different factor or a different argument). The first sentence should set out what this idea is, then other sentences either explain and develop the point further or give an example or evidence. It's also a good idea to finish with a sentence recapping the main point you have been trying to make.

Senka

Putting in supporting evidence is really important because the exam is all about using sources as evidence! Make sure that every time you introduce an idea into your answer you can back it up with a short quote from the sources or some extra knowledge that you have revised.

Marcus

You need an introduction and conclusion because these are the places where you can set out your overall ideas about the question – in the introduction, what you think the question means, definitions of key words and a summary of your argument. The conclusion summarises your main argument and is a place where you can spend time improving the interpretation you have been given.

Harry

I took a 50/50 approach to revision. I spent half the time learning all the key information – the usual stuff – so I knew my facts in the exam. The other half of my revision concentrated on skills, because I knew that I was going to be assessed on my ability to work with sources. I practised reading sources, writing paragraphs about their strengths and weaknesses, devising my own hypotheses. I made sure I knew how I needed to approach the questions as well as background information.

Hayley

I wanted to make sure that I knew exactly what the exam was going to be like. My teacher made sure we had a copy of the specification so we could see what topics might come up. I checked the OCR website and there was some good stuff on there – like mark schemes and examiners' reports that gave me more clues about what I needed to do to get a good mark. I also got copies of past papers and checked the timing and then practised like mad!

Ammar

I got really, really bored just reading my notes over and over again, so I decided to put everything onto my PC. Then I made some powerpoints about each topic. Typing it all out, deciding what to put in and what I could safely leave out, and setting up all the pages with layouts, animations and so on actually made the facts start to stick. When my friends found out what I had done they actually offered to buy the powerpoints off me! When I revise for next year's exams I might check out podcasts so I can carry my notes round with me on my iPod!

Alex

I like to make mind-maps of the topics we have covered, the more colourful the better. I can remember the shape of the mind-maps and that helps me to recall the information I've written on them. Using lots of colours, sketches and doodles helps as well. I can visualise the mind-map better if I've taken trouble to design it.

Jo

I get into a panic if I leave revision to the last minute; I like to draw up a plan so that I can cover all the topics in good time. I don't go as far as setting out what to do each day because I can never stick to that, but I do set myself a target for each week. I set small targets because I really feel I've achieved something when I've completed them.

Refresh your memory

Getting started...

Creating an interrogation dossier

The historian has to enquire into what has happened and the only way to do this is to use the evidence. Questions have to be asked of the evidence in order to find out how reliable and useful the evidence is. A source that is not reliable may still be useful.

Your first task is to draw up a list of questions that you can use when evaluating sources. Divide a page of A4 in two, or use a double page spread in an exercise book, and set out the questions under the following headings:

1) Content/context/situation

These are questions that relate to what the source shows or says, the background to the production of the source and the position or situation of the author of the source when the source was produced.

▷ When was the source produced?
▷ Was there censorship at the time?
▷ Was the author in a position to know what happened?

2) Purpose/nature

These will be questions that relate to reasons why the source was produced and its form; whether it is a painting, a cartoon or an extract from a diary, letter, newspaper or whatever.

▷ Is the source propaganda?
▷ Does the author attempt to distort the evidence?
▷ Is the extract drawn as a piece of satire?

The more questions you come up with, the better your evaluation of the sources will be.

Revision checklist

Key issue 1: Why was the First Crusade launched?

▷ The boundaries of medieval Europe on the eve of the crusade, including the Muslim world, the Holy Roman Empire and the Byzantine Empire.

▷ The reforms the papacy underwent in the period 1073–95 and the importance of the Investiture Contest.

▷ The motives of Pope Urban II in launching the First Crusade and the appeal from Emperor Alexius.

▷ The significance of the pilgrimage in the medieval mind up to 1095.

▷ The concept of Holy War and how the pilgrimage became the 'armed pilgrimage' where the killing of non-Christians was encouraged and rewarded by the Church.

Key issue 2: Why was the First Crusade successful?

▷ The mass appeal of the crusade to the common people and to the military classes.

▷ The importance of the leaders such as Godfrey of Bouillon, Baldwin of Boulogne, Raymond of Toulouse and Bohemond of Antioch.

▷ The response of the Byzantine emperor.

▷ The military victories in the East; the Battle of Dorylaeum, the capture of Edessa and the siege of Antioch.

▷ The divisions within the Muslim world that left the Muslims unprepared to repel the crusaders.

▷ The capture of Jerusalem and the slaughter of its inhabitants.

Key issue 3: Assess the reasons for the development and survival of the crusader states in the twelfth century

▷ The establishment of the kingdom of Jerusalem and the diminishing papal and Byzantine influence.

▷ The crusaders' territorial gains along the coast.

▷ The development of the crusader states of Antioch, Edessa and Tripoli.

▷ The importance of castles in defending the new kingdom.

▷ The importance of the new military orders of the Knights Hospitallers and Templars in defending the kingdom.

▷ The continued weakness and divisions within the Muslim world.

Key issue 4: Assess the causes, course and consequences of the Second Crusade

▷ The reasons for the fall of Edessa in 1144; the significance of Zengi and crusader weaknesses.

▷ The response of the West; Pope Eugenius' call for a crusade, St Bernard's preaching.

▷ The leadership of Louis VII of France and Conrad of Germany.

▷ The reasons why the Second Crusade failed to recapture Edessa and why it attempted to capture Damascus.

▷ Consequences of the divisions between the western leaders and growing strength of the Muslim forces for the crusader kingdom.

Key issue 5: Assess the causes, course and consequences of the Third Crusade

▷ Long-term problems such as the lack of manpower, the weakness of King Baldwin IV (the leper king) and the failure to capture Egypt; the significance of Nur ad-Din and the rise of Saladin from 1174.

▷ The short-term causes including the political weaknesses in the kingdom, such as the death of Baldwin V and the accession of Guy; the struggle for power between the war-party (Reynald of Chatillon and the Templars) and the peace-party (Raymond of Tripoli).

▷ The Battle of Hattin and the fall of Jerusalem in 1187.

▷ The preparations of Richard I of England and Philip of France and the significance of the death of Emperor Frederick Barbarossa.

▷ The political divisions between Richard and Philip; Philip's early departure and Conrad of Montferrat's murder.

▷ The victories at Acre and Arsuf and the reasons why Richard failed to recapture Jerusalem.

Key issue 6: How and why did the reaction of the Muslim world to the creation and existence of the crusader states change during the twelfth century?

▷ The significance of the notion of the jihad after the First Crusade.

▷ The importance of Nur ad-Din's achievements.

▷ The growing power of Saladin and the unification of Egypt, Damascus and Syria against the crusader kingdom.

▷ Changing relations between Christian settlers and Muslims.

Key ideas/Questions

Here are some important ideas to think about while you are writing:

▷ How significant were the papal reforms and ideas of Holy War?

▷ Why did so many people join the crusade?

▷ Was it Muslim disunity or crusader faith that made the First Crusade successful?

▷ How secure was the new kingdom in 1130?

▷ How did the failure of the Second Crusade contribute to the declining security of the kingdom after 1148?

▷ Was it Saladin's success or the crusaders' mistakes that led to the fall of Jerusalem in 1187?

▷ How significant was the jihad in the growing Muslim unity between 1148 and 1187?

▷ Why was Richard I unable to recapture Jerusalem?

Get the result!

The Historical Enquiries paper

Remember that on the Historical Enquiries paper you will be faced with two questions.

The (a) question will always ask you to compare two sources as evidence for something. It is worth 30 marks and you should spend roughly 30 minutes on this question.

That leaves you 60 minutes to deal with the (b) question, which requires you to use all the sources and your own knowledge, and is worth 70 marks.

(a) questions

▷ You should spend 30 minutes on this answer. Make sure you spend 5–10 minutes planning. Once you know the significant areas of agreement and disagreement, it will not take long to write the answer.

▷ You do not need to complicate things. Keep your answer clear and focused. The key to getting a top mark is writing about **why** the sources differ/agree, not how they differ/agree, so do not stick with just a basic comparison.

▷ Begin with a point-by-point comparison, dealing with the sources together, not separately, to make a proper comparison.

▷ Use short quotations to reinforce your points, but use your own words to explain the points of comparison.

▷ Always look to compare the sources as evidence for something, which is what the question will require of you.

▷ Remember that you do not need to use any of your own knowledge explicitly in this question, but you will need to know the context of both sources in order to evaluate them effectively (i.e. what was happening in that year, what happened just before, who the author is and who the recipient of the source is). Think about the situation and purpose of the author and the audience, and look at the date of the source. These issues may well explain the tone and the language used in the source.

Structuring your answer to (a) questions

▷ The first two paragraphs are comprehension-style accounts of the similarities and differences between the two sources, but make sure you stick to the focus of the question (comparing them as evidence for something).

▷ The third paragraph, which is the key paragraph, examines the provenance of the sources and why they agree/disagree (situation, purpose and tone).

▷ Finally, you need to make a judgement in your conclusion as to which of the sources provides the better evidence for what you have been asked. This might be because one source is limited in some way in terms of its provenance or content.

Sample (a) question: the motives of the crusaders

Study Sources A and B.

Compare these sources as evidence for the reasons why people went on the First Crusade.

Sources

 A

Until now you have fought unjust wars; you have often savagely brandished your spears at each other in mutual carnage only out of greed and pride, for which you deserve eternal destruction and the certain ruin of damnation! Now we are proposing that you should fight wars which contain the glorious reward of martyrdom, in which you can gain the title of present and eternal glory.

From Guibert of Nogent (before 1108), describing Urban's speech at Clermont in 1095 and how he criticised the civil wars between Christian warriors

 B

If the knights of other provinces have decided with one mind to go to the aid of the Asian Church and to liberate their brothers from the tyranny of the Saracens, so ought you with one mind and with our encouragement to work with greater endurance to help a church so near you resist the invasions of the Saracens. No one must doubt that if he dies on this expedition for the love of God and his brothers his sins will surely be forgiven and he will gain a share of eternal life through the most compassionate mercy of our God.

Pope Urban to the knights of Besalu, Empurias, Rousillon and Ceradaña, 1096–99

Sample answers

Examiner says:

The candidate makes a good start in analysing the sources together, not separately, and using short quotations.

Alex's answer

▷ Both Sources A and B agree on the heavenly rewards the crusaders will get if people go and fight the Muslims. They will be rewarded with 'eternal glory' (Source A) and 'eternal life' (Source B). In Source B, Urban is offering to forgive the sins of anyone who dies on the expedition and in Source A they will get the reward of martyrdom when they fight the wars. The sources differ in that they do not present much unity between the knights. In Source B, the knights of 'other provinces' have decided to go and liberate the Christians from the 'tyranny' of the Muslims but in Source A the Pope is criticising the knights for fighting one another in 'unjust wars', fought out of greed and pride with very severely damaging effects. In Source A Urban suggests that not only will eternal glory be offered for those crusaders but also 'present' glory, implying that the crusade will win them honour and prestige on earth.

The sources differ in their purpose and provenance. Source A is an extract from Pope Urban's speech at Clermont in November 1095, as recorded by Guibert of Nogent, one of several accounts of Urban's speech. There is no surviving account of Urban's speech and the various accounts differ slightly. Guibert's account was written before 1108 and is therefore within a range of thirteen years from the actual event. However, it is clear what the purpose of Urban's speech was and this was to stir up religious hatred and galvanise the masses into armed action against the Muslims. Urban's speech was a carefully prepared piece of propaganda, using warrior-like language to condemn their civil wars and turn them towards Islam. Their previous wars have been 'unjust' whereas the wars against the infidel will be just. There is also a threat there of 'eternal destruction' and 'ruin and damnation' for these civil wars, which can be saved by going on the crusade where 'present and eternal glory' will be offered. The attraction of 'present' glory is important, because Urban needs as many people to go on the crusade as possible, the knights in particular who can win prestige and reputation by going on the crusade.

Source B is a letter from the Pope to a specific group of knights with a more specific date range (1096–99). This is after the 1095 call for the crusade at Clermont and is again a source from Pope Urban, but as a letter is more direct evidence rather than a secondary recording by Guibert. Urban here is appealing directly to the knights of one area in France rather than to the masses in Source A. The tone and the language are softer and less critical than Source A. He mentions the knights of the 'other provinces' who have gone to the crusade as a means of persuading these

Examiner says:

The candidate continues an excellent answer by assessing the provenance of both sources and using this to explain differences between them.

knights to join the crusade, perhaps making them feel guilty for not going yet. He does not mention any unjust civil wars.

In conclusion, both sources are useful evidence for the reasons why people took the cross. Eternal glory and the forgiveness of sins are explicitly mentioned by Urban, who is the source of both extracts. They differ in tone and language because of their audience and Source A is perhaps more limited evidence as it is not directly from Urban but from Guibert of Nogent, who may have written it from memory years later and after the success of the First Crusade.

(b) questions

You have left yourself 1 hour to complete the (b) question, which is worth 70 marks. Make sure you leave 10 minutes to plan your answer and to think about which sources agree/disagree with the statement and why that might be the case. The object of the (b) question is to assess how far the sources, with your own knowledge, support an interpretation.

▷ Highlight the focus of the question and shape your argument around it. Remember that you have to consistently assess how far the sources support the interpretation.

▷ Group the sources around the focus of the question, so that your approach is analytical, rather than source by source (for example, 'Sources B and D support the interpretation but A and C to a lesser extent if at all').

▷ Remember to evaluate the provenance and reliability of source material as you go along.

▷ Keep the sense of argument or debate throughout your answer rather than surveying the sources.

▷ Use short quotations from the sources to illustrate your points, but always explain the point in your own words.

▷ Integrate your own knowledge as you go along, rather than 'bolting on' a paragraph at the end. Bring in issues or events that are not included in the sources, as long as they are relevant to your argument which refers to the interpretation you are assessing. Do not write a paragraph which is purely knowledge-based and goes off at a tangent to the question, but do use the sources as a means of using your knowledge to explain the events and issues. Keep it short, sharp and relevant.

▷ Form a balanced judgement on the question in light of the sources.

Writing a plan

▷ Draw up a table of two columns, one column for sources that agree with the question and one for sources that disagree.

▷ Fit each source to a column. Some sources might fit both columns because they are ambiguous or implicitly support the interpretation. You must, however, include every source in the table.

▷ Highlight some key quotations from each source to show how it fits your argument. Use different colours to highlight 'agrees' and 'disagrees', so that you can see them at a glance while you are writing.

▷ Add points of evaluation to your plan. Look carefully at each author and date. Think about the provenance of each source (you will have done this already for two of the sources in the (a) question). Ask yourself **why** the author was writing, **who** they were writing for and whether they were in a **position** to know about the issue. Look at the language, tone and perspective of the author and how they relate to the content.

▷ Add some relevant knowledge to your plan. This will be information that builds on what is in the sources, expanding on an event or person – maybe the author or recipient – and it will be information that cannot be found in the sources. It may support the sources or may oppose what the sources say in relation to the interpretation you are assessing as a whole. Integrate your information to your argument, rather than putting it at the end.

Structuring your answer

▷ Make a judgement in the first sentence on 'how far' the sources and your knowledge support the interpretation (e.g. four out of the five sources support the view, therefore they support it to a great extent). Set out arguments both in favour of and against the interpretation in the introduction, grouping the sources into those which support/those which oppose the interpretation

▷ Then, write about those sources which support the interpretation, evaluating their provenance and purpose – bringing in your own knowledge relating to that source and the wider context; finish by prioritising those sources which are the strongest and most informative.

▷ Next, write about those sources which oppose the interpretation, again evaluating provenance and purpose – bringing in your own knowledge relating to that source and the wider context; finish by prioritising those sources which are the strongest and most informative.

▷ Conclusion: return to the question and reinforce the original point about how far the sources support/oppose the interpretation (your judgement), using extra knowledge of your own outside the sources and anything you omitted earlier on.

Sample (b) question: the nature of warfare in the crusader kingdom, 1100–30

Study all the sources.

Use your own knowledge to assess how far Sources A to E support the interpretation that castles were the most significant reason for developing crusader military power in the period 1100–30.

Sources

(A) **Walter the Chancellor, writing 1114–22, an eyewitness from the Principality of Antioch**

The Muslim tactic was to draw the crusader forces out into a single battle and defeat them. The crusaders were constantly short of men and had to wait for reinforcements before committing to battle, if at all.

Therefore the Persians [i.e. Muslims] marvelled that a race so ready for war and always intolerant of injury, who had been provoked so often by arrows, afflicted so often by jeers, was so long-suffering, because the Christians did not signal the start of battle and were already submitting as if fear had conquered them. Some of our men even considered it an act of cowardice; however some of greater perspicacity interpreted it as the purpose of the prince [Roger of Antioch] so that, when he was sure the time was right, they would be stronger to attack, not at the enemy's summoning, nor in anticipation of their forces, but by the prudent disposition and enormous experience of himself and the king …

(B) **Fulcher of Chartres, *History of the Expedition to Jerusalem* (written 1127)**

Fulcher describes a stand-off between Christian and Muslim armies in 1118.

There assembled a very large army of horsemen and infantry with the intention of destroying the Christians of Jerusalem in battle. Tughtigin, the King of Damascus, advanced to aid them with his men. Then King Baldwin of Jerusalem with the men of Antioch hurried off to do battle against the hostile army. But because each side greatly feared to attack the other, for nearly three months both sides managed to postpone fighting for reasons of this kind. Then the Muslims, worn out by the delay, abandoned the war.

(C) **William of Tyre, writing in the 1180s**

William describes the gradual encirclement of Muslim-held Ascalon in the 1140s by crusader castles.

Our people resolved to erect fortifications around about [Ascalon]. Within these strongholds forces could easily be assembled which, from their very proximity, would check the enemy's forays. Such fortresses would serve as bases to make frequent attacks upon the city itself. Often by themselves, more often in company with men at arms from the other fortresses built with similar intent, these men issued forth to encounter and defeat the enemy when they tried to make raids from the city. The whole district became much more secure because the locality was occupied and a more abundant supply of food for the surrounding country was made possible.

(D) ***In praise of the New Knighthood*, Bernard of Clairvaux, c.1130**

When the battle is at hand, they arm themselves inwardly with faith and outwardly with steel rather than with decorations of gold, since their business is to strike fear in the enemy rather than to incite cupidity. No matter how outnumbered they are never awed by the fierce enemy hordes. Nor do they overestimate their own strength, but trust in the Lord to grant them victory.

(E) **J. Phillips, *The Crusades, 1095–1197* (2002)**

While battles could exert a decisive influence on Frankish power, the key to holding on to territory was the control of castles and fortified sites, which included towns and rural manor houses. The knowledge gained in the course of the [First] crusade proved invaluable in taking the other castles and fortifications of the Levant, as the Franks established their rule. It was then the settlers who had to refortify, develop and construct their own defences in order to preserve their hold on the Holy Land and to provide centres of authority.

Sam's answer

Castles were a significant reason for the developing military power in the Kingdom of Jerusalem, but not necessarily the most significant reason. Other factors, such as victory in battle and Muslim disunity were equally, if not more, significant. Only two of the five sources (C and E) support the view that castles were the most significant reason, but Sources A, B and D suggest that battle, delaying tactics, Muslim lack of interest and sheer faith were just as important. Four of the five sources are primary sources, though Source C is actually near contemporary, written forty years after the events described but by a resident of the Holy Land and a well-respected historian. The secondary source, historian Jonathan Phillips, makes a judgement that castles provided the 'key' to holding on to power.

The importance of castles in reinforcing and controlling an area is illustrated in Source C, William of Tyre, where he describes the way in which crusader castles encircled Muslim-held Ascalon. The castles, probably timber, were easily assembled and served several purposes. First, they could 'check the enemy's forays' meaning that they could limit the raids the besieged could make from the town, for supplies as well as for attacking the crusaders. Secondly, the ring of castles could attack Ascalon itself; the source clearly states that the ring of forts co-operated to defeat the enemy. In this way, the whole area was 'much more secure' because the food supplies and the villages were occupied by crusading forces as a result of this ringwork of besieging forts. Siege warfare was a major feature of medieval warfare and had played a large part in the success of the First Crusade, where Antioch and Jerusalem had fallen to sieges. Source C demonstrates that the gradual, piecemeal occupation of the region successfully consolidated the new crusader kingdom. However, it may be said that Source C has limitations, firstly because it was written forty years after the fall of Ascalon in the

Examiner says:

This is a good introduction with a sense of overall judgement focused on the question. The sources are grouped analytically to assess the interpretation and their provenance is referred to early on.

1180s, during the high point of the crusader kingdom when the author may be trying to justify or at least glorify the crusader success. He may also be trying to create a better sense of unity within the kingdom by emphasising the cooperation between the crusaders in capturing Ascalon. William of Tyre was chancellor of the kingdom and therefore had access to the documents and records of the kingdom, which certainly affirms his reliability.

Source E is the other source which supports the interpretation that castles were the most significant reason in the developing crusading power. It is a secondary source where the author is making a judgement. He says that although battles could exert a 'decisive' influence on crusader power, it was the building of castles that provided the key to holding onto power, therefore agreeing with Source C. Castles not only secured the particular position but also the towns and rural manor houses and they then provided centres of authority. Law courts, taxation records and money could be stored securely and criminals imprisoned in the new castles. Garrisons could ride out quickly and effectively into the region in a show of force when necessary and the villagers could seek refuge within the walls.

Source E does however say that battles could exert 'decisive' influence and Sources A and B certainly support this rather than the view that castles were the most significant factor. Both were written by contemporary eyewitnesses and agree that battles could be so important that avoiding battle was almost as important as risking a battle. In Source A it is clear that the crusaders are not yet established enough to risk a single battle, despite the provocation of Muslim arrows and jeers. The Prince of Antioch, Roger, was clearly waiting for the moment when he was strong enough to attack, such was the risk of battle. The source is dated between 1114 and 1122, but we know that Prince Roger was in fact killed in the notorious battle 'of the Field of Blood' in 1119 when the entire Antiochene armed forces were wiped out and Roger's head was sent to the caliph in Baghdad. Although the battle was catastrophic, the king of Jerusalem, Baldwin II, came to the aid of Antioch and prevented the region falling to the Muslims, which demonstrates that even such a battle as this was not necessarily decisive.

Source B agrees with Source A on the nature of the risk entailed by a single battle. Indeed it says that both sides feared battle so much that they postponed fighting, unlike in Source A where the crusaders fear battle more. Even though the king of Damascus, Tughtigin, has a 'very large' army, the Muslims are eventually worn out by the delay and abandon the war. This illustrates the strength of the crusaders in that all they had to do was sit tight and fight a defensive war rather than put all their armies into battle. Fulcher, like Walter, was a contemporary writer, but he was not an eyewitness whereas Walter was; he is also writing nine years after the event, but nevertheless he provides a useful and reliable account which largely agrees with Source A and does not support the interpretation that castles were the most significant reason for developing crusader power; indeed, neither Source A or B actually mention castles or siege warfare.

Source D makes no mention of castles either; Bernard of Clairvaux talks about the power of inward 'faith' during battle and outward 'steel' and suggests that however much outnumbered the Christians are in battle, it is their faith – their 'trust in the Lord' which will grant them the victory. Faith played a major part in crusader success – and it was the reason why they were in the Holy Land in the first place – and the success of the First Crusade, both the sieges and battles, were all attributed to God's mercy and God's divine power and blessing, a contemporary belief we cannot divorce from our assessment and understanding of military achievements. However, St Bernard's view does not chime with the other contemporary sources which highlight the risks of battle. Indeed, St Bernard was a monk and theologian who never visited the Holy Land and never witnessed battle. He was writing the source as a tool to justify and incite violence committed by Christians, and in this case, for the new military order of the Knights Templars, founded in 1119, probably as a result of the Battle of the Field of Blood that year. St Bernard wrote a Rule for them and created a new type of knighthood, those fighting monks who personified the just war. Therefore, Source D is limited in providing eyewitness contemporary evidence for the nature of both castle and battles in the developing crusader military power.

Examiner says:

These are good paragraphs. They convey a sense of argument, reinforce points with short quotations and address the provenance of the sources, integrating some own knowledge and cross-referencing the sources. The answer successfully contextualises the source material and makes some excellent observations on the nature and purpose of the sources.

In conclusion, the sources are divided on the significance of the castle. Battles could be decisive and very risky and so were avoided if at all possible. None of the sources refer to the lack of Muslim unity in this period, which was a key reason for the success of the First Crusade. Gradually, and after some victories, especially the Battle of the Field of Blood in 1119, the Muslim world began to unite under the banner of the jihad, the Islamic version of the holy war. Source A certainly suggests that the Muslims were confident enough by 1114–22 to provoke the crusaders into battle and Source B tells us that Tughtigin assembled a 'very large' army of horsemen and infantry in 1118. But the failure of the Muslims to unite under one leader of the whole region, rather than the local sultans and atabegs, was a major factor for the continuing survival of the crusader kingdom, not mentioned by any of the sources, all of which are written from a western perspective. In truth, it was a combination of castles, victory in battles, Muslim weaknesses and diplomatic alliances which gradually strengthened the crusader kingdom.

The Period Studies paper

'Religious zeal was the main motive of those who went on the First Crusade.' How far do you agree with this view?

It can be argued that to a great extent, religious zeal was indeed the main motive of those who went on the First Crusade. However, it was not the only motive, as there were several key reasons why people answered Pope Urban's call to holy war in November 1095, including political, social and economic reasons. Each of these factors, and the leaders who collaborated with Urban, needs to be examined in order to make an assessment as to the main motive.

Urban preached at Clermont in November 1095 and at the end of the council he launched his extraordinary and almost revolutionary call to arms. He exaggerated the persecution of the Christians in the Holy Land by the 'infidels', although in fact pilgrims were allowed access to the holy sites and the Byzantine empire had staged a solid defence of their borders in Asia Minor since the disastrous defeat at Manzikert in 1071. As well as whipping up 'war fever,' Urban offered remission of sins to those who took up the cross to go to defend the holy churches (Jerusalem was mentioned but quickly became the focus of the crusade, so potent a force was it in the medieval mind). Remission of sins for going on an 'armed pilgrimage' was a radical, if not revolutionary, step away from the Christian principle of 'love thy neighbour'. Urban was asking people to kill for God; war would become a form of prayer, a penitential act, which would gain the crusaders their place in Heaven and eternal bliss.

The response to Urban's call was massive and unprecedented, never to be repeated in such numbers. It is suggested that 60,000 people set off in the summer of 1096 and this was after the so-called 'People's Crusade' led by Peter the Hermit, consisting of many thousands of mainly non-combatants. Religious zeal in response to Urban's call was undoubtedly the main motive of most people. Life was nasty, short and brutish in eleventh-century Europe, with an average life expectancy of 30 years, 50% infant mortality and years of back-breaking toil on the land. The medieval mind was steeped in religious devotion at all levels and all times. Any education was religious; any reward to the everyday life was purely spiritual in that the aim on earth was to get to heaven through prayer, penance and religious devotion; the pilgrimage was an obvious means of doing this.

Urban knew full well that he was drawing on an ancient tradition of pilgrimage. For centuries, people had trekked to Jerusalem and the holy sites as well as Rome, as a form of penance and to gain remission for their sins. But Urban had his own, political, motives; he did not necessarily want unarmed peasants walking to Jerusalem, but he did need an army to go on a military mission to conquer the area and keep it. Therefore although the call to arms was steeped in religious zealotry, in reality, Urban's political needs were greater.

Pope Urban's excuse came from the Byzantine emperor, Alexius, in a letter sent in March 1095. Alexius asked for troops, probably a few thousand, to help defend the eastern empire. Urban saw this as an opportunity to launch a holy war and go way beyond Alexius' request. Urban was himself a product of the Cluny abbey and part of the reform movement the papacy had established since the 1050s, including Alexander II, who had blessed William the Conqueror's invasion of England in 1066 and Gregory VII, who had clashed with the German Emperor Henry at Canossa in 1076, forcing him to submit to the new papal demands of political power in Europe. By launching a holy war in 1095, Urban could take the political leadership of Europe one step further.

Urban's speech at Clermont was very carefully orchestrated and part of a propaganda campaign which included targeting the leaders of the Frankish nobility such as Godfrey of Bouillon and his brother Baldwin, Hugh of Vermandois, Raymond of Toulouse and Stephen of Blois. These nobles undoubtedly agreed to come — and bring with them thousands of troops bound by their feudal loyalty — for religious reasons, but there was a clear political motive too and that was to create a new kingdom in the Holy Land answerable to the pope in Rome — not the emperor in Byzantium. Urban was himself a member of the nobility and understood the codes of conduct in a warrior society; his speeches are full of references to the 'knights of Christ' (milites Christi) and the 'belt of knighthood', deliberately appealing to the honour and the warlike aspects of his audience. The crusade would, therefore, be a military expedition with political objectives. Several of the leaders, such as Baldwin, Godfrey and Raymond, had no intention of returning, as they were going not only for religious zeal but for the new kingdom they would carve out in God's name. Baldwin became the first King of Jerusalem in 1100.

There were social and economic reasons as to why so many took the cross. The landholding elite were limited by the system of primogeniture, whereby the eldest son inherited the estate, leaving his younger brothers to fend for themselves. Physical labour was not an option, though entering the Church was, though families with seven or eight sons could not send them all to the Church. This problem was worsened by a population boom in northwest Europe in the later eleventh century, but the Norman Conquest of England in 1066 and Norman colonisation of southern Italy, where a new kingdom was created by 1100, partly solved this problem. The feudal ties of obligation often meant that entire groups of young men set off to the Holy Land after 1095 in search of the 'land of milk and honey' which Urban had offered. As well as settlement, booty and plunder were the temptations and the Norman warlords. Bohemond and Tancred are classic examples of this type of crusader (Bohemond went no further than Antioch in 1098, establishing his principality there).

That said, the motivation of booty and plunder did not pay off. Two thirds of the crusaders died en route; many mortgaged their estates to raise the money to go in the first place, leaving their families in danger of attack, although the Church promised protection. The overwhelming motivation for most crusaders was the remission of sins offered by Urban at Clermont. Everyone knew that the journey would be a difficult and dangerous one, even in peacetime circumstances (a high-profile casualty was Robert, Duke of Normandy, William the Conqueror's father — he had died on the journey in 1035). It is clear from the sources of the time that taking the cross was a perilous mission and most did not expect to return.

In conclusion, Pope Urban's campaign in 1095 was designed to appeal to certain members of society to achieve his political aims. The military and political motives of the crusade leaders and their feudal hosts was significant, but it was the religious passion which swept across Europe that motivated people first and foremost, overwhelming Urban and Emperor Alexius. The tradition of pilgrimage, war fever and propaganda and a sense of apocalypse as the century drew to a close, coupled with full remissions of sins and entry to Heaven was the main motive for most people and would be the potent force behind the success of the crusade in 1099, ending in the slaughter of the inhabitants of Jerusalem in 1099.

Examiner says:

A good survey of the other factors and motives which puts the religious zeal into context and supports the argument made at the beginning.

Examiner says:

A very good answer, strongly argued and supported with excellent knowledge, clearly set out from the beginning, though perhaps with some lack of clarity in the first few paragraphs before a closer focus is established on the crusaders', rather than the papal, motives.

Bibliography

Asbridge, T.S. (2004). *The First Crusade: a new history*. UK: Simon and Schuster.

Bennett, M. (2006). *Fighting techniques of the medieval world AD 500 to AD 1500*. New York: St Martin's Press.

Erdmann, C. (1977). *The origin of the idea of crusade*. Princeton, N.J.: Princeton University Press.

Hindley, G. (2007). *Saladin: hero of Islam*. Barnsley: Pen & Sword Military.

Lacey, R. and Danzinger, D. (1999). *The year 1000: what life was like at the turn of the first millennium: an Englishman's world*. Boston: Little, Brown.

Maalouf, A. (1984). *The Crusades through Arab eyes*. London: Al Saqi Books, distributed by Zed Books.

Mayer, H.E. (1988). *The Crusades*. New York: Oxford University Press.

Nicolle, D. and Hook, C. (2003). *The First Crusade, 1096–99: conquest of the Holy Land*. Oxford: Osprey.

Nicolle, D. and Hook, C. (2006). *The Third Crusade, 1191: Richard the Lionheart, Saladin and the struggle for Jerusalem*. Oxford: Osprey.

Peters, E. (1971). *The First Crusade; the chronicle of Fulcher of Chartres and other source materials*. Philadelphia: University of Pennsylvania Press.

Phillips, J. (2002). *The Crusades, 1095–1197*. Harlow: Longman.

Reston, J. (2001). *Warriors of God: Richard the Lionheart and Saladin in the Third Crusade*. New York; Toronto: Doubleday.

Richard, J. (1999). *The Crusades, c. 1071–c. 1291*. Cambridge, England; New York, NY: Cambridge University Press.

Riley-Smith, J.S.C. (1986). *The first crusade and the idea of crusading*. London: Athlone.

Runciman, S. (1955). *A History of the Crusades*. Cambridge: Cambridge University Press.

Smail, R.C. (1956). *Crusading warfare, 1097–1193*. Cambridge: Cambridge University Press.

Tyerman, C. (2006). *God's war: a new history of the Crusades*. Cambridge, MA: Belknap Press of Harvard University Press.

Glossary

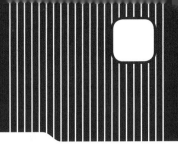

amirs, atabegs Titles of the local Turkish chieftains and rulers.

anti-Semitic Showing hostility or prejudice towards Jews (Semites). Attacks, or pogroms, fired hatred towards the Jews of central Europe which raged on and off for hundreds of years, reaching a dreadful climax in the Holocaust in the twentieth century.

caliph A Muslim religious and political leader. The caliphs were Muhammad's successors.

confess Each week, or more often if possible, medieval people would attend confession: they went to see a priest and told him about their evil or ungodly deeds or thoughts. The priest would forgive people's sins on God's behalf, often setting them some sort of punishment or penance.

doge In the republics of Venice and Genoa, the elected head of state.

enfeoff The act of granting land from the king or a nobleman to a knight was called enfeoffment. The land granted by this act was commonly known as a fief. The ceremony was sometimes recorded in writing, but more often than not it was witnessed by people representing both sides of the agreement. A clod of earth, to represent the land, was passed from one to the other. The new holder swore an oath to serve his lord in return for the land.

Genoese Genoa was a city-state in northern Italy. It grew wealthy on maritime trade and had a powerful navy.

hajj The pilgrimage to Mecca, in Arabia. Mecca is important to Muslims as the town where Muhammad proclaimed the new Islamic religion. Every able-bodied Muslim who can afford it must complete this journey at least once in their lifetime.

hereditary Titles and land were inherited in the Middle Ages. A man could acquire land by marriage, but it was rare to marry an heiress without being of the same social status and level of wealth. Intermarriage preserved the elite class of landowners and passed on land from father to son by inheritance. If a man died without sons, then his nephews, brothers or cousins inherited.

Holy Lance The lance that pierced the side of Christ during the crucifixion.

Holy Land The region that included Jerusalem – the Holy City where Jesus was crucified – and the towns of Bethlehem and Nazareth, plus the areas of Jordan and Galilee. All were held in high esteem by the Christian West.

hospice In medieval times, a lodging for travellers and pilgrims, run by a religious order.

indulgence In the medieval Catholic church, a reduction of or exemption from punishment for sins committed during one's life.

knight The knights were the class of warriors who held land from the king and the church.

mining A technique for bringing down sections of a castle or town wall. The besiegers would dig away the earth at the foot of the wall until they could tunnel underneath. They would put in wooden props to support their tunnel, then withdraw and set light to the props. The wall above would usually collapse at this point. Mining could be dangerous work for the diggers: their tunnel might collapse, and they were a sitting target for the defenders on the top of the wall.

ordeal by fire In medieval times, a person's innocence was often tested by subjecting them to ordeals such as walking through fire or being submerged in water. If they survived, this was taken as God's proof of their innocence.

paganism Before the existence of Christianity, people in **Europe** worshipped many gods – gods of the air, fire, water and earth. Only when Christianity became the official religion of the Roman Empire in the early fourth century did paganism begin to decline. After the Roman Empire collapsed, Europe reverted to paganism again, but Rome itself remained Christian and by AD 700 the church had succeeded in converting the pagans across Europe.

papal bull An official order from the pope.

patriarch A senior Christian bishop in one of the most ancient cities (Rome, Constantinople, Alexandria Antioch and Jerusalem).

penance It was believed that after death, entry to heaven was only granted to those whose souls were the purest. Purity was gained through acts of penance such as prayer, devotion to good works, and pilgrimages. All these increased a person's chances of getting to heaven.

primogeniture In northern France, only the eldest son inherited the family lands. Other sons got nothing. They could go into the church, marry an heiress or join a nobleman's household as a soldier. In this way, the family estate remained intact, rather than being divided amongst

many brothers. A woman could only inherit her father's property if there were no male heirs, including cousins, which was rare.

rapine Violent theft of another person's property.

razed When something, usually a building, is completely demolished.

relic A religious object such as the bones or clothes of a saint, or even part of the cross on which Jesus was crucified (the 'True Cross'). Touching or kissing a relic was believed to cure illness and cleanse sins. Holy relics were stored in ornate boxes known as reliquaries. If an oath was sworn over one of these it made the oath even more binding.

remission of sins In Christianity, a priest's formal pronouncement of forgiveness of the sins of a person who has expressed repentance. For the crusaders, the act of taking the cross and going on the crusade was an expression of repentance.

squires Young men, sometimes teenagers from noble families, who cleaned the knights' weapons and tended their war-horses. Each knight had with him several squires, who would ride into battle close behind their lord. In time, the squires would expect to be knighted and find a position in a great nobleman's household, or be granted land of their own to live off.

tonsure Monks all had a distinctive haircut which shaved the middle of the head, leaving a fringe all around.

vassal A vassal was subject to an overlord within the feudal structure that governed medieval society. He could be a landless peasant owing allegiance and farm-labouring duties to the local lord of the manor, or he could be a mighty prince swearing allegiance to an emperor to whom he owed military service. The greater the vassal, the more knights he usually provided to his lord.

Viking A general term applied to the pagan warriors who sailed from Norway, Sweden and Denmark to pillage, plunder and raid the wealthy and peaceful lands of France and England from the end of the eighth century to the early eleventh century. Some settled in northern France from 911, and their (Christian) descendants were the Normans who eventually conquered England in 1066.

vizier In some Muslim countries, a high-ranking government official, the chief counsellor to a caliph.

Index